BLACK
AND
PRESBYTERIAN

BOOKS BY GAYRAUD S. WILMORE

Black and Presbyterian:
   The Heritage and the Hope

Last Things First

The Secular Relevance of the Church

BLACK AND PRESBYTERIAN

The Heritage and the Hope

BY

GAYRAUD S. WILMORE

Published for
Black Presbyterians United
by

THE GENEVA PRESS
PHILADELPHIA

Copyright © 1983 Gayraud S. Wilmore

BOOK DESIGN BY DOROTHY ALDEN SMITH

First edition

Published by The Geneva Press®
Philadelphia, Pennsylvania

PRINTED IN THE UNITED STATES OF AMERICA
9 8 7 6 5 4 3 2 1

Library of Congress Cataloging in Publication Data

Wilmore, Gayraud S.
  Black and Presbyterian.

  Expansion of lectures delivered at San Francisco
Theological Seminary, San Anselmo, Calif., May 1980.
  Bibliography: p.
  1. Afro-American Presbyterians.   2. Afro-Americans—
Religion.   3. Afro-American churches. I. Black
Presbyterians United.   II. Title.
BX8946.A35W54 1983   285'.1'08996073   82-23907
ISBN 0-664-24440-8 (pbk.)

Contents

Foreword

The idea for this book came out of a lively conversation between the author and a group of ministers and seminary students in California. In May 1980, Gayraud S. Wilmore was the commencement speaker at San Francisco Theological Seminary in San Anselmo. Taking advantage of his presence on the West Coast, I and a group of Black clergy and seminarians arranged to have him remain over for a few days to lead us in some reflection and discussion about Black Presbyterians—who are we, where did we come from, what do we hope for in this church? At the end of the conference we talked about a book on the subject. Professor Wilmore roughed out an outline on the plane back to Rochester and after it had been circulated among some West Coast leaders of Black Presbyterians United we agreed that the book should be written and made available to the entire Presbyterian family as soon as possible.

What follows in these pages is essentially an expansion of the lectures given at San Anselmo. Professor Wilmore lays out in clear and concise language the meaning of the Black religious experience, but particularly the pain and agony, joys and exhilarations, of being a Black Presbyterian. His treatment of the history of Blacks in the Presbyterian Church is brief, but refreshing and informative. The enigmas and contradictions related to our presence within this predominantly white church are candidly faced. Professor Wilmore explores the reasons why Black believers, despite all the problems, would not be denied the opportunity to witness to Jesus Christ as Savior and Liberator through the instrumentality of a predominantly white and often racist institution.

This book has relevance for the discussion now going on in several denominations about the role and status of Black members. Laypeople and clergy within the United Church of Christ, the United Methodist Church, the Disciples of Christ, the Episcopal Church, the American Baptist Churches, and other denominations will find that the issues raised here are all too familiar. White Christians in these denominations, as well as within Presbyterianism, will learn how better to relate to Black brothers and sisters, and to the members of other ethnic groups, by reading and discussing this book.

A variety of purposes are served by the publication of this book at this time: It will contribute to the celebration of the 175th anniversary of Black Presbyterianism in the United States by reminding us of the rich history of our involvement in the denomination; it will provide a study and discussion resource for laity around the meaning of Black culture, the theological insights that arise from our journey, and the identity crisis which Black middle-class Christians are facing in this post-civil rights period; it will make some valuable suggestions about how Black Christians generally, and Black Presbyterians particularly, ought to be relating to the Black communities around the country of which they are a part.

This book, in short, should help Black Presbyterians get in touch with themselves as they reflect upon their history and the mission they should be about today. Others who read these pages will learn of the sacrifices and gifts of Blacks to the life and development of Presbyterianism in the United States at a time when the merger of its two largest branches is anticipated and all Presbyterians need to appreciate what the Afro-American constituency has contributed to and what it demands from the new united Church.

This book was commissioned by Black Presbyterians United

and its publication made possible, in part, by a generous gift
from one of its friends of long standing. Black Presbyterians
United, the national caucus of the denomination, extends its
heartfelt thanks to Gayraud S. Wilmore for presenting to the
Presbyterian family—lay and clergy, at home and abroad—a
challenging study worthy of consideration by every member of
the denomination as we all strive for the "unity within
diversity" that God wills for the whole Church of Christ.

CLAUDE C. KILGORE

National President,
Black Presbyterians United,
Los Angeles, California

Introduction

This is a true story. The names have been changed, as they say, to protect the innocent, or the guilty—depending upon how you look at it. It actually happened to someone I know, and telling it here at the very beginning should help to get our discussion started, because it illustrates the major issue with which this book deals, indeed, why it was written in the first place.

Inez Jones was baptized when she was twelve years old in the pool of Ebenezer Baptist Church in the middle of the Black community of her city. But Inez and Tom Jones decided to join the First Presbyterian Church because it was just down the tree-shaded street from the beautiful new house they bought in the suburbs in 1975. It was not an easy decision. The Joneses knew absolutely nothing about the Presbyterian Church. And on top of that, it was—as far as they could tell on Sunday mornings—entirely *white!*

They probably would have gone back into town every Sunday to old Ebenezer, but the minister at First Church was one of those youthful fiftyish, blond, blue-eyed bombshells. What a contrast, they remarked almost in the same breath after he left their house the first time, to the sainted but weary old warrior, Rev. Isaiah Robinson, back at Ebenezer. The last time Reverend Robinson had been in their home was when Tom's Aunt Fanny died and Tom was responsible for the arrangements. That was four years ago. The minister of First

Church called on them at least once a week for two months, had the men's fellowship invite Tom to a softball game with St. Paul's Episcopal, and sent two women elders, who happened to live in her block, around to give Inez a double welcome—"to our church and to our neighborhood." Rev. Peter Manning just would not give up and, in the end, he got the Joneses. "Two good young Baptists gone to lettin' somebody tamper with their religion," as Inez's mother snorted when she heard about it.

Tom wasn't much of a churchgoer. About every other week he had some excuse ready by Saturday night. But Inez always believed in being active in anything she belonged to. She was destined to being no different at First Pres than she had been at Ebenezer. Every Sunday worship service, the midweek sewing club, the special Lenten Bible study group, and—before the end of her second year—first chair in the alto section of the senior choir.

I have to skip some of the details of what brought her to the attention of Rev. Clyde Homer, the presbytery executive, but it happened, as you might guess, through the intervention of the irrepressible Pete Manning, her pastor. There is no question about it. Any church executive who has to fill a dozen committee slots with intelligent laypeople would have had difficulty passing up Inez Jones. In two years she became more than casually knowledgeable about the Presbyterian Church, although her Black friends downtown could never have guessed it. She was not the kind to boast about a new interest, but she read a couple of library books on Presbyterian history, a manual for church members, and almost every word of A.D. when it arrived in her mailbox once a month.

Reverend Homer asked her if she were elected would she serve on the Board of Trustees for Mulberry Manor, the presbytery's home for the aged. Inez, with her usual enthusiasm, said yes and to no one's surprise she was elected at the January 1977 meeting of the presbytery. With characteristic seriousness she read all the minutes and annual reports

Reverend Homer could supply her with in preparation for her first meeting.

I don't remember exactly what triggered it, but it came sometime toward the end of her first six months on the Mulberry Manor board. In the middle of a monthly meeting, in the midst of a discussion about the disposition of a windfall bequest that one of the recently departed residents had left to the home, while everyone was shuffling papers trying to find next year's budget projection, Inez suddenly asked herself: What am I doing here?

That night she talked it over with Tom, who listened sympathetically but had little advice to offer. Tom was a college classmate of my youngest brother and he suggested that they open up the subject with me the next time I happened to be in town. My brother got the word to me and the opportunity came in the spring of 1978.

"I really have to ask myself," she said, when the three of us met for dinner at my hotel, "what I am supposed to be doing on that board—maybe even in the Presbyterian Church."

"Boards of trustees can be boring," I punned.

"It isn't that, at all. It has to do with not being sure about my role. I mean, what *I* have to contribute—if anything. Mulberry Manor never had a Black resident in all its seventy-five-year history, and from my visits over there I don't know any Black person who would want to be a resident—much less could afford it. You know—eighty-year-old white ladies. They have some Black maids and yardmen, but nobody on that board would ever think about integrating the professional staff. The residents are nice enough people, I guess, but neither they nor the board think about integrating the clientele. Should I worry about it? Did Rev. Homer get me on for that purpose? Maybe he hasn't even noticed that I'm a Black woman.

"You know, it's just like at First Church. Tom and I can't tell whether we're Rev. Manning's 'Exhibits A and B,' his token Negroes, an excuse for calling First Church integrated, or whether he really wants us there like any other newcomer on our street, and would be embarrassed if we said anything about wishing there were more Black folks in the congregation.

"But is that a good attitude for us to have? I mean, is that *Christian*—to want to see more of your own folks—if it's O.K. to put it that way?" She gave a little nervous laugh. "You all must know what I mean. I guess I could just forget that I'm Black and be a good, ordinary member of First Presbyterian and the board of the old folks' home—putting my two cents in like anybody else. And yet most of the congregation and the members of the board haven't given a thought to getting Black people to join, probably wouldn't push the idea anyway. And wouldn't have the foggiest notion about how to do it if they wanted to. So where does that leave me, huh? I think sometimes that I'm really overanxious about wanting them to face up to something that I can't even explain myself. But that's not why Tom and I joined First Church, is it, Tom? Oh, God—am I confused!"

Inez Jones's story is not an unfamiliar one to anyone who is an alert and reflective member of a predominantly white denomination like The United Presbyterian Church in the U.S.A. or the Presbyterian Church in the U.S.—the two largest branches of Presbyterianism in the United States. But Black Episcopalians, United Methodists, American Baptists, Unitarians, members of the Reformed Church in America, the Congregational Church, the Disciples, and Black Roman Catholics have all had similar experiences. Many of us who work in these and other denominations that are predominantly white have talked about the etiology of Inez's "confusion." We have been calling what she went through an *identity crisis*. Having one is the first step in moving from confusion to clarity, from sickness to health. It is like a fever that must be induced and broken, sometimes artificially, before the patient can get well.

This book is about the identity of Black people in the

Presbyterian Church. It attempts to address such questions as what it means to be Black *and* Christian, or Black *and* Presbyterian and involved, like Inez Jones, in a lay ministry within a structure dominated by whites, most of whom have never related to nonwhites as equals and often send out confusing signals to sensitive Black church members.

But do not expect to find all the answers here. Our purpose is not so much to produce irrefutable answers as to stimulate reflection and discussion by laypersons like Tom and Inez Jones—and, as surprising as it may seem, by whites like Pete Manning, their pastor, Reverend Homer, the presbytery executive, and the good (and perhaps not so good) people of the First Presbyterian Church and the board of the presbytery's home for the aged. How do we plan to go about this?

We begin with the assumption, which few knowledgeable people will challenge, that in institutions like the Presbyterian Church, where Blacks comprise a minority of less than five percent, most of whom worship in "separate" congregations, there are many problems that make mockery of Paul's words to the church in Galatia: "There is neither Jew nor Greek, there is neither slave nor free, there is neither male nor female; for you are all one in Christ Jesus" (Gal. 3:28). There are not only racial and class prejudices—on both sides—but more subtle problems arising from patterns of institutionalized racism of long standing—paternalism and servile self-abnegation, apathy and repressed anger, ignorance and cynical nonparticipation, underrepresentation and the consequent underutilization of gifts. But even more difficult than the problem of betraying, in these and other ways, our given unity in Christ, is the problem of the *nature* of that unity. How *should* Blacks and whites be together in the same church, assuming that that is the will of God and given the history of racial oppression in the American churches and in the nation?

Our second assumption is that Blacks, on their part, do not come to such a discussion without valuable resources of their own—resources that arise from Black history and culture, from what is called the Afro-American religious heritage and the particular perspective from which Black people individually and in groups, such as Black Presbyterians United (BPU), look at God's activity in today's world and try to deploy themselves to meet and work with him for the redemption of the world. Chapters 2, 3, and 5 will attempt to restate and examine that heritage and perspective. We are particularly interested to ask what they have to say to Black Christians like Tom and Inez Jones, but also to laypersons who have continued to belong to all-Black congregations, who have never, or rarely, experienced interracial worship, and have never been invited to join a presbytery committee!

Our third and final assumption has to do with you, the reader. We assume that every Christian is, in a rudimentary sense, a theologian—one who tries to think and talk about God in an orderly, intelligent fashion.

Since the best theology is that which is done in dialogue with others—whether believers who knew Jesus personally or had a special relationship to the early church and left us their writings, or scholars and theologians who write books, or friends who gather together in someone's home to begin a study group—it is through encountering, evaluating, and synthesizing the ideas and experiences of others, under the guidance of the Holy Spirit, that greater truth breaks forth. We hope that all of the above forms of dialogue will come into use as you wrestle with the ideas of this book. The most desirable form for dealing with what you will find here is, of course, a congregational study group, where common prayer, the Scriptures, other books and articles, and a variety of helps and resources can be used to supplement the opinions of the participants. For that purpose we have included at the back of this book not only questions for reflection and discussion but a list of nontechnical books and other resources which lay readers may wish to consult for arriving at a more considered judgment.

A word more needs to be said about the Scripture texts which begin each chapter. This familiar practice for books of sermons should not be taken to imply that in this book what follows is a formal exposition or sermonic treatment of the passages. That was not our intention. Rather, you should regard these texts as the flags or banners one often sees these days festooning the sanctuary. The texts provide a mood, an enveloping atmosphere for prayerful reflection, a Biblical backdrop for the historical and theological material in each chapter. This kind of Biblical ambience needs to be a part of the study of each chapter.

Our suggestion is that the group leader first read the Biblical texts and ask whether members of the group found anything in the chapter that hinted at why the author chose those particular texts. Do they seem to have some application to the position taken in the chapter? If so, how would group members describe that application—or misapplication? What do the passages suggest in the minds of group members that is relevant to the problems and issues being explored?

The group may then want to turn to the questions at the back of this book and begin the discussion looking for connections between them and the recommended texts. In other words, every effort should be made to use the Bible along with this book. The Black Church has always been a Bible-centered church. It has not been slavish about it, but creative and imaginative in its use of Scripture. This discussion of the heritage and the hope of Black Presbyterians should continue the tradition it speaks about by making the Bible central to our search for the meaning and significance of our pilgrimage.

It may be, after all is said and done, that it does not really matter what Black Presbyterians think about their heritage and what they hope for in the Presbyterian Church. They may continue to be an underrepresented constituency—blandly ignored and amiably oppressed in this church—and would do better by transferring their membership to a Black Baptist, Methodist, or Pentecostal denomination. Those are, after all, the churches that approximately eighty-five percent of Black Christians in the United States call home. If that is the direction in which God is leading his Presbyterian children of African ancestry, we hope these discussions will help to clarify the reason for that choice and we submit to his will. If, on the other hand, Paul's statement to the Galatians is still in effect and we have only to trust the Holy Spirit, remain in this predominantly white church, and come to some agreement about the unity we seek, then perhaps this book will serve that purpose at least as well. Perhaps it will help Black believers to understand the crisis many of them are experiencing today in white churches and ecumenical agencies, on this side of much-too-facile assumptions about integration in the civil rights period of the 1960s. And if we all understand the reasons for our discomfiture and find a new religious and cultural vocation for liberating ourselves and others from the asphyxiating strictures of racism, then we will realize a oneness in Christ that is not one-sided and impoverished, but full-orbed, luxuriant, and overflowing with the promise that he came to fulfill in his church and in all humankind.

So, then, let us begin our search.

1
On Being Human—
In General and in Particular

Genesis 1:27
Acts 2:6–11
Galatians 3:28

Contrary to popular opinion, believing in the *imago Dei*—the Christian doctrine that all men and women are created in the image of God—has nothing to do with whether or not one believes in scientific creationism or evolution. It is, perhaps, much easier for creationists who take the Bible literally than for those who believe that our prehistoric ancestors emerged from the primal oceans millions of years ago as aquatic mammals and roamed the East African forests as apes millions more, before becoming what we would call human. But some evolutionists have held on to the idea of being created in the image of a divine Creator by sanctifying the principle of life itself, whether in an earthworm or an Einstein, and seeing in the climb up the ladder of evolution, from simple to more complex forms of life, the gravitational pull of the perfection which is the Creator.

We Can Still Begin with the Bible

Both points of view—scientific creationism and evolution—are theories rather than absolute, unquestionable facts. In both cases it is more a matter of believing than knowing for sure. But even more important for our purposes is that whichever view you prefer, it is still possible to take the Bible seriously and affirm that the first chapter of Genesis reveals a profound truth about who we are as living beings—and upon whom our destiny depends.

In other words, unless we just want to do so, there is no reason why we need to get into a fight at this point about whether or not we have to scrap the Bible to talk intelligently about being human. Our point of view is decidedly affirmative about the Biblical story of the creation of the first man and woman. Indeed, we would argue that it is not possible to understand fully what it means to be a human being apart from the Genesis story in its mythological totality, and further, apart from the life, death, and resurrection of Jesus Christ. But by the use of that much maligned word "mythological," we have already telegraphed the fact that we read the Biblical story of creation more as sublime poetry, more as the teaching of ancient wisdom for living, than as the factual account of an event that one might expect to find reported in this morning's *New York Times*.

"In the image of God he created him; male and female he created them." There is no mention of white or Black; Jew, Christian, or Muslim; Asian, African, or North American. Those are categories that have no immediate significance for what is going on here—the essential calling of the creature who is named man/woman. This does not mean, mind you, that those other categories do not have some significance in other contexts. It only means that at *this* level—on "the bottom line," as they say—whatever were the scientific details of our coming into concrete existence, it was *God* who called us into the consciousness of being the creature man/woman who had no other identity except to be identified with, in, and for each other and with, in, and for God. Thus, Gen. 2:24 says, "And they became one flesh," and 2:7, "The LORD God . . . breathed into his nostrils the breath of life; and man became a living being," which is another way of saying that the very life of God is a part of our intrinsic being. We godlike creatures were made for one another and can only exist in community and cooperation with one another.

The Image of God Defaced

Beyond that, the Bible goes on to stimulate our most creative thinking about the meaning of life with ancient stories concerning the origin and earliest development of human society: the problem of alienation and fratricide in the Cain and Abel story, the wickedness of humankind and its destruction in the story of Noah and the Flood, God's covenant with the survivors and the division of the races, the story of the Tower of Babel. In these mythological sagas out of the civilization of the ancient Near East, touched with the fire of divine inspiration, we are invited to ponder ageless questions, to explore some of the most realistic and yet the most exalted explanations ever conceived for addressing the fundamental dilemmas of human nature and experience.

At the core of this way of thinking about life and human history is, of course, the story of Adam and Eve—the point at which the whole drama begins to unfold. The temptation, the Fall, the expulsion from Eden, provide a basic framework for focusing our attention on what is and has always been wrong with us—individually and collectively. It is in the act of human willfulness and autonomy, which the story of Adam and Eve uncovers, that the image of God—that indefinable quality stamped upon our human natures which makes us "a little lower than the angels" and justifies our responsible stewardship of the earth—becomes defaced. A fatal flaw breaks out like an inexorable disease, a deep-seated acne upon our human *persona* obscuring and distorting our godlikeness. And now we are capable of the most demonic and monstrous behavior which can no longer be called human—behavior that we see performed in the genocide of native Americans at the beginning of our country, in the Atlantic slave trade, in the Holocaust, and in countless other ways and by many people, every day of our lives.

It is not therefore, on prima facie evidence, absolutely

incontrovertible that humanity is human! Being human is not so simple a matter as being a man or a woman—reasoning, planning, proposing, and all the other marvelous things you and I do that supposedly make us superior to other forms of life. If the Bible is trustworthy in what it tells us about the humanity with which we were created and its subsequent corruption, then humanity, in the strictest sense, is not something already possessed by anybody but something to be struggled for, something to be achieved against internal and external forces working in the opposite direction in our lives. It is not "to be or not to be" that is the question, but how to *become* human. That is a question with which the Bible is intensely interested and one that it answers more satisfactorily than all the simplistic rhetoric of the creationists or the intricate speculations of the evolutionists.

We do, of course, speak casually about being already human, and what ought to be the case about this or that—for example, food, shelter, and a decent job—because we are human beings and need a certain level of those necessities in order to live a human life. But that is only a manner of speaking—useful, perhaps, but not precise enough from a Biblical, particularly a New Testament, standpoint. When the apostle Paul writes, "We know that the whole creation has been groaning in travail together until now; and not only the creation, but we ourselves" (Rom. 8:22–23), he is speaking of the incompleteness of all things because of sin. Neither nature nor humankind is what it should, in itself, have become. We human beings groan inwardly, waiting for our humanity which Paul calls our "adoption as sons, the redemption of our bodies." And John tells us that the true pattern for our humanity is Jesus Christ. While we are not certain about all that that means, we at least know that we lack the fullness of that humanity and yearn for its fulfillment.

> Beloved, we are God's children now; it does not yet appear what we shall be, but we know that when he appears we shall be like him. (I John 3:2)

So we can only speak of being human beings with a certain amount of poetic license. We would wish that we were and that everyone else in this world were human in the way that Jesus was and is! That would be a different kind of world indeed.

Jesus Was a Particular Human—So Are You

The church's great confession, dating from the fourth century A.D., is that Jesus of Nazareth was fully God and fully man. As the Nicene Creed puts it: "begotten, not made, being of one substance with the Father . . . was incarnate by the Holy Spirit of the Virgin Mary, *and was made man.*" But it is in the New Testament itself that we find unmistakable confirmation of the "historicity" of Jesus—his personhood as a human being, "one who in every respect has been tempted as we are, yet without sin" (Heb. 4:15), set in the context of human history, even as we are. The writers of the Gospels make us see that Jesus was human not only in the general sense of that term—eating and drinking, becoming annoyed with the Pharisees, weeping over the death of Lazarus, suffering and dying—but that he was a *particular* human being. For when you really think about it, there is no such thing as a human being in general. Each one of us is a particular human being, a unique person. It should not surprise us that the New Testament picture we have of Jesus is of a first-century Jew, born in Bethlehem of Judea, brought up without noteworthy honor in Nazareth of Galilee, who began his public ministry sometime during "the fifteenth year of the reign of Tiberius Caesar, Pontius Pilate being governor of Judea, and Herod being tetrarch of Galilee" (Luke 3:1). He was a historical being, a particular personality with a particular identity. That fact is hammered home again and again by the New Testament writers. Matthew and Luke go so far as to include lengthy genealogies of Jesus' family (Matt. 1:1–17; Luke 3:23–38) just to be doubly certain that we do not make the mistake of thinking of him as some kind of disembodied spirit, some heavenly representative of a generalized humanity, but not what the dudes on the corner used to call "a meat man."

Down through history it has been difficult for some people to accept the fact that Jesus was a Jew, a member of a despised group, a pariah people who have been the object of prejudice and discrimination for countless generations. It would have been better, some Gentiles have speculated, if Jesus had been born a German like Martin Luther, or an Englishman like Sir Thomas More—or even an Italian, like most of the popes. But a Jew? We cannot, however, get away from the eyewitnesses that our Lord and Savior was a Jewish young man, circumcised as an infant on the eighth day, presented at the Temple with "a pair of turtledoves, or two young pigeons" according to the law of Moses, and committed in every way to the religion and culture of his people.

Indeed, while we know that in the end Jesus meant his gospel to be for the salvation of all people—"to the Jew first and also to the Greek" as Paul would say (Rom. 1:16)—in the beginning of his ministry he understood himself to be sent only among his own people. As strange as it may seem, we have an interesting story in Matthew 15 and Mark 7, in which Jesus says to the Gentile woman who entreats him to heal her daughter something to this effect: "My ministry is supposed to be exclusively designed for the Jewish people. I am not disposed to waste the precious gifts given to me on people outside of our Jewish community" (Matt. 15:21–28).

We know that the faith of those who were not Jews put the faith of Jesus' own people to shame, for a prophet is not without honor except in his own country and among his kith and kin. And in The Acts of the Apostles we see that the gospel went out from Jerusalem to the rest of Judea, to Samaria, and to the ends of the earth. Paul and the apostles recognized that Jesus was a Savior not only of the Jews who believed in him but of all who would believe—in every race and nation, male as well as female, bond as well as free.

But the message of the Kingdom of God had to begin somewhere before it could be disseminated everywhere. It had to originate in the life, death, and resurrection of a particular person, in a particular time and place, and among a particular people, before it could become the universal Word of Life for the redemption of the world. For life has concreteness and specificity—every leaf of grass, every bird or flower is alive in its own unique individuality—despite the fact that modern biology and medicine have demonstrated that we all have parts that are interchangeable with the parts of certain others; note that this is particularly true of members of the same family. But it is precisely because the messenger had a specific identity and particularity that the message has a universal appeal to each of us and to all people of every nationality and period of history.

Because of the selfhood, individuality, and particularity of Jesus we know that God respects our selfhood too, that he accepts our particularity. We too were born at a specific place and time, of a particular biological inheritance and socialized to a particular culture. No one needs to be ashamed of that. Who and what we are as candidates for the status of humanity, as the provisional human beings we would like to be, is inseparable from the particularities of our existence—whatever they may be—expressed in family background, gender, race, nationality, time and place.

Some Blacks have had the experience of a white person saying to them, after becoming acquainted or having become fast friends: "You know, I just never think of you as being a Negro anymore. I really don't notice your color, or the shape of your lips or nose. I have actually become color-blind where you are concerned."

We all know what such a person means to say. We might even agree that it would be better if people were not embarrassed, or shocked, or made to feel disgust or threat at the way someone else appears to them. Yet we all want to be taken for what we are—creatures made in the image of God—and not have that which is a part of us, our color, race, nationality, or gender, cast aside as if it were only an unfortunate excrescence and that the pure, undefiled you or me were hidden somewhere inside. Our humanity, if we can now use that word with a somewhat better understanding, is bound up with our genetic and cultural characteristics. It is not that it is impossible or undesirable to overcome backgrounds or change cultures. It is, rather, that everyone must begin somewhere in order to become the broad, cosmopolitan person we might wish to be, and it is a matter of good sense, as well as dignity and self-esteem, to begin with who we are in the identity given to us by our parents and significant others. For through the agency of those closely related to our birth and development in our individual particularity, God impressed something of himself upon each of us. The image of God is related to us through our self-identity and self-consciousness as transmitted to us by other persons in a particular historical context.

The second birth, our incorporation into Jesus Christ through baptism, began a new identity for us. We took on his name as *Christians*. But even in this new relationship to him and to others called by the same name, we do not totally lose our historic particularity. He does not barge into our existence and carelessly dispose of everything we possess as human beings—color, race, family background, and gender, even as superficial as some of these may seem to be. Rather, he transforms and employs all these gifts for his new family, the church, so that we can "grow up in every way into him who is the head" (Eph. 4:15).

All One Body We

"All one body we," but with significant differences, for which we can all be grateful. A rose garden can be very beautiful, and all of us enjoy seeing a Christmas tree with ornaments of all one color, shape, and size. But too much homogeneity for too long a period is not only boring, it can be positively dangerous, as psychologists can demonstrate in prisons and psychiatric hospitals, and geneticists support in studies of the close mating of related individuals. Charity begins at home, but variety is the spice of life—if we can bring together two old sayings that almost sound like nonsense when put together, but illustrate what we are trying to say in this and the previous section about ethnic particularity and Christian pluralism.

In other words, it does not contradict what the New Testament tells us about our oneness in Jesus Christ to talk about and even celebrate our differences. We have not always believed that. During the 1950s America went through a period when it was considered bad taste, and possibly unchristian, to emphasize racial and cultural differences. That is still the case in some countries where radical diversities and tribalism threaten to tear the nation apart. But we are far from that in the United States. Nevertheless, during the 1950s people attending interracial seminars on prejudice and race relations institutes emphasized what he or she had in common with everyone else. We searched for uniformities. "All one body we" meant melting down all idiosyncratic aspects and attitudes of Christians until all became practically interchangeable around the Father's throne—un-self-aware, color-blind, and deracinated little automatons—praising God with one voice on a single note. Sometime later, in the 1960s perhaps, we found that the hymns we were singing were conceived, composed, and set to an arrangement by and for only that part of the family who were born and raised in a certain setting, with certain cultural assumptions and certain understandings of history not shared by all God's children in America. What was presumed to be optimum integration turned out for many to be the worst kind of cultural imperialism—the subservience of everything Black to everything white. The superficiality of that solution to the problem of our disunity was evident in the fact that the one-way integration of the Christian community, in the few places where it could be demonstrated, ceased at the front door of the workshop, or summer conference, or congregation where we had come together. Not only were we obliged to repress our ethnicity—a part of each person's humanity—for the sake of a false integrationism, but once we reentered the world outside we could no longer rely upon that alternative vision of how things ought to be. Every race was again on its own—and Blacks were expected to take the back seats and be quiet about it.

Does this mean that the essential meaning of the search for a truer, more Christlike humanity is in our differentness, in our separate races, nationalities, and cultures? Does it mean that somehow the whole human family seen as a whole from a distance, as one might view our solar system from a nearby star, is a unity, but when it comes to a close encounter, one gets a more realistic picture by concentrating more on the differences than on the similarities, the polarities rather than the sameness? Not exactly. Here again, if we want to talk about realism and yet take fullest account of the possibilities of exceeding our ordinary expectations, we must turn to the Scriptures.

The Tower of Babel and Pentecost

In the story of the Tower of Babel in Genesis we have a profound myth of human disorder and alienation. We cannot take the time here to explore all the interesting and enlightening facets and sidelights of Gen. 11:1–9, for whole books have been written on that brief passage and no one has ever exhausted its possibilities. But the core of what is being said is that because of the arrogance of human ambitions and the determination of humankind to take matters into its own hands, God scattered the various peoples and nations in the particular parts of the earth where each predominated. God decreed a confusion of tongues so that they "may not understand one another's speech" and would abandon the project to build a city whose tower reached into the heavens and challenged the sovereignty of God.

> Therefore its name was called Babel, because there the LORD confused the language of all the earth; and from there the LORD scattered them abroad over the face of all the earth. (Gen. 11:9)

From that point on, the Bible assumes that the plans and projections of humanity are doomed to failure. With many languages rather than one, as after the time of the Flood, it is impossible for the various nations of the earth to understand one another sufficiently to pool their intelligence and resources and achieve the greatness of which they were otherwise capable. Moreover, they were scattered abroad in various regions, hopelessly out of touch not only by speech but by geography. It is a further sign of the disobedience and sin of our ancestors and of us, their descendants, that we can build nothing enduring together because of an ancient predisposition to alienation and divisiveness. Here, then, is heterogeneity to a tragic fault—a superabundant pluralism that is counterproductive for world progress and peace. We are forever frustrated because of our racial and ethnic differences. Our suspicions and lack of mutual understanding continually breed incoherence and noncooperation.

Little else is said about the separation of the nations (we may read "races" or "nationalities") in the Old Testament. The Jews, God's chosen nation, are to be the agents by whom all the families of the earth will someday be blessed. And the time would come, or so taught the prophets, when those outside of Judaism would seek the Lord and humankind would be permitted to make that "name for itself" which was denied at Babel.

Let not the foreigner who has joined himself
    to the LORD say,
     "The LORD will surely separate me from
      his people";
and let not the eunuch say,
    "Behold, I am a dry tree."
For thus says the LORD:
"To the eunuchs who keep my sabbaths,
    who choose the things that please me and
     hold fast my covenant,
I will give in my house and within my walls
    a monument and a name
    better than sons and daughters;
I will give them an everlasting name
    which shall not be cut off.

"And the foreigners who join themselves to
    the LORD . . .
these I will bring to my holy mountain,
    and make them joyful in my house of
     prayer; . . .
for my house shall be called a house of
    prayer
    for all peoples."

                    (Isa. 56:3–7)

Behold my servant, whom I uphold,
    my chosen, in whom my soul delights;
I have put my Spirit upon him,
    he will bring forth justice to the na-
     tions. . . .
He will not fail or be discouraged
    till he has established justice in the earth;
    and the coastlands wait for his law.
                    (Isa. 42:1–4)

The divisions of the peoples of the world will be brought to
an end when the word goes forth that God has brought
salvation to all humankind. As the prophets foretold, God will

now gather all the nations with their various languages unto himself, and thus also to one another.

> Many peoples and strong nations shall come to seek the LORD of hosts in Jerusalem, and to entreat the favor of the LORD. Thus says the LORD of hosts: In those days ten men from the nations of every tongue shall take hold of the robe of a Jew, saying, "Let us go with you, for we have heard that God is with you." (Zech. 8:22–23)

The writers of the New Testament recognized in the statements concerning the coming Messiah prophecies of the life and work of Jesus, who would bring all people together under the Kingship of the God of Abraham, Isaac, and Jacob. The Lord's Servant or Messenger, of whom many of the Old Testament prophets wrote, will establish a new covenant when he comes and will end the alienation and confusion of Babel in the universal worship at Jerusalem. All people will acknowledge and worship him, for he will establish righteousness and justice in the earth.

The supreme resolution of the problem of Babel is Pentecost, when the disciples of Jesus returned to Jerusalem, as he commanded before his ascension, and "were all together in one place." On that day the Christian church was born, and almost immediately it began to extend its boundaries beyond the Jewish community of Palestine to every race and nation in the known world.

In the account in Acts 2, Luke clearly makes the point that the effects of Babel are reversed at Pentecost. What we have experienced as separateness and alienation, symbolized by the attempt to "make a name for ourselves" at Babel, is overcome and reversed in the proclamation of the name of Jesus, the risen Lord, to the international community which is attracted to a certain house in Jerusalem where the disciples poured out their hearts in miraculous manifestations of the Holy Spirit.

And they were amazed and wondered, saying, "Are not all these who are speaking Galileans? And how is it that we hear, each of us in his own native language? Parthians and Medes and Elamites and residents of Mesopotamia, Judea and Cappadocia, Pontus and Asia, Phrygia and Pamphylia, Egypt and parts of Libya belonging to Cyrene, and visitors from Rome, both Jews and proselytes, Cretans and Arabians, we hear them telling in our own tongues the mighty works of God." (Acts 2:7-11)

Most of these were undoubtedly Jews, but the passage tells us that some were devout Gentiles. All of them, Jews and non-Jews alike, heard the word of God in the language of the lands from whence they came—diverse places in Asia, Africa, and Europe. Although the story of Pentecost is usually taken, in this respect, to indicate that racial and cultural divisions are superseded by the common experience of the Holy Spirit who confirms the truth of the message of Jesus to all people alike, it should also be noted that the confirmation is given in the particular language of each group. There is no attempt here to lift up one language or culture, be it Hebrew, Greek, or some other, as having exclusive priority as the channel of God's grace on this memorable occasion. The evangelist has something important to say to us by this fact.

Pentecost is indeed the symbol of our unity in Jesus Christ by the power of the Holy Spirit. But it is also a wonderful testimony to the validity of cultural pluralism. God did not choose to repudiate or disqualify our cultural and ethnic differences, represented in Acts 2:7-11 by the list of the regions of the known world and the variety of languages in which the gospel might be communicated. The very opposite is the case. The particular cultural and ethnic differences that seem to have been a curse at Babel now become a means of blessing, serving the evangelical purpose of the Holy Spirit at Pentecost. God honors our differences when they are offered to him in love and faith. He uses them for the propagation of the gospel, the building up of the church, the extension of his Kingdom among all the peoples of the earth.

What We Owe to Ourselves and to Each Other

Our search for humanity really begins with hearing the gospel in the context of our own peoplehood and cultural identity, but we can only become human after we recognize what God is doing in the peoplehood and cultural heritage of others and realize our own incompleteness without their experience. It should be obvious that this is something different from saying: "Our various backgrounds, languages, and cultures only serve to divide us. We must get rid of them and submit to one common culture—the *Christian* culture—and then we can be faithful to the gospel."

It usually happens that the dominant group determines what shall be considered "Christian culture" and all others are expected to adapt their own orientations and life-styles accordingly. As we shall see, in the United States (but also in Africa and the Caribbean) this means that Afro-American Christians were expected to become carbon copies of Euro-American Christians, and gradually to lose their peculiar ways of worshiping God in order to become "normal Christians." Black church leaders of the eighteenth and nineteenth centuries refused to accept this one-sided interpretation of Christianity and we had, as a result, the historic development of African Baptist and African Methodist churches in both the New World and Africa.

The problem continues to plague many Christians today. Some of us drifted into a predominantly white denomination, like Tom and Inez Jones, because it was convenient and we were made to feel welcome. But some of the rest of us left Black and came over into white denominations because we were somehow persuaded to believe that here is where authentic Christianity was to be found, that the white churches provided the most appropriate rallying ground, the legitimate baseline around which all other groups—at least in the United States—should be integrated if we are to discover what it really means to be one "chosen race," one "royal priesthood," one "holy nation" in Jesus Christ (I Peter 2:9).

But if becoming human, properly speaking, and becoming Christian, properly speaking, are very nearly one and the same thing, then neither is possible by giving up the inheritance we all bring from the past and subsuming everything under the supposedly superior qualifications of white, Anglo-Saxon, North Atlantic Christianity. As the apostle Paul says, quoting the psalmist:

> None is righteous, no, not one;
> no one understands, no one seeks for God.
> All have turned aside, together they have
>   gone wrong;
> no one does good, not even one.
>   (Rom. 3:10–12)

It is not so much that there are no differences worth respecting between one approach to the faith and another, or that all are of the same quality; the point is that none is *perfect*. All forms of humanity are corrupt and all interpretations of the faith are flawed. If we are serious about our religion, we must be prepared to engage one another in a common search for a truer humanity than any of us have ever known, for a restoration of the face of Jesus Christ upon our own disfigured countenances. But that can only happen as we bring whatever God has endowed us with in our ethnic particularity to the common table of his children of many colors, races, languages, and cultures, there to see the reflection of our truer selves in the mirror of another's eyes. We, in other words, contribute our best to others for their growth and development as human beings when we, in turn, recognize in them what we need in order to become better human beings ourselves. There are no one-way streets. The traffic is going both ways.

People become human as they encounter and relate to one another out of their own selfhood and peoplehood, giving freely and humbly to others and appropriating from them that which they lack in themselves.

The church of Jesus Christ is a microcosm of the family of humankind. Not only is it the place where all the families of the earth can finally lay claim to the promise made to Abraham (Gen. 12:3), but insofar as it seeks to be conformed to the mind and spirit of Christ, its head, the church too is in quest of true humanity—the vanguard of all who are traveling through history in that same direction. Just as we cannot become genuine human beings by surrendering our individuality completely to others, or overstressing it to the exclusion of others, we cannot become authentically Christian by renouncing our ethnic and cultural backgrounds completely on that account, or by presuming that our inheritance has some God-given priority over other groups and cultures. If many white Christians have committed the latter sin, many Black Christians have committed the former—particularly those of us in the Presbyterian Church.

Let us put the matter squarely. Some of us have been so anxious to prove to our white brothers and sisters that we too are Americans and that we too "belong" that we have deprived them of the gifts God has given to us as a people. Too few of us know anything about these gifts—and that is one of the reasons for this book. We have been so busy learning how to be "human beings in general" that we have paid little attention to the special qualities of Black humanity that we have to bring when we are true to our own history and traditions. We cannot be human beings in some general, nonspecific way, and God will hold us accountable for depriving other members of the human family of the fullness of their calling to be human beings.

But that is not the end of the matter! We cannot achieve what we desire in this Presbyterian Church—a valid and satisfying experience of Christian discipleship—until we respect and acknowledge our particularity, until we involve ourselves in the theological and cultural interchange that helps us all "attain to the unity of the faith and of the knowledge of the Son of God, to mature humanity, to the measure of the stature of the fulness of Christ" (Eph. 4:13).

In the next chapter we will look at the experiences that Black people in America have brought to the Christian religion. Not until we know something about Black church history as a whole will be able to evaluate critically and appreciate the best of the particular contribution of Black Presbyterians.

2
What Is Black Christianity?

Joshua 4:4–7
Acts 4:13
John 8:36

The first problem we must address is one of terminology. The idea of a Black or a white Christianity is offensive to many people and we may as well deal with their objections at the very beginning.

Sometimes one hears the question: "What does the Bible have to do with a Black Christianity or a white Christianity? Show me those terms in Scripture and we'll have something to talk about—otherwise I will have nothing to do with either one."

Such a requirement is, of course, impossible to satisfy and the discussion must come to an end before it begins. The word "Christian" appears only three times in the Bible (Acts 11:26; 26:28; and I Peter 4:16) and "Christianity"—with or without a modifier—never. It is a term used to describe the religion that developed around the person and work of Jesus of Nazareth, long after both he and those who knew him in the flesh had passed off the scene. When you and I use the term "Christianity" we are speaking, whether we know it or not, as sociologists of religion—that is to say, as persons interested in the belief systems, practices, and social structural aspects of this tradition. If someone says, "Not me. I have no such interests," I can only reply, "Well, in any case, that's what the word refers to most precisely whether you're interested in such things or not."

Both in ordinary conversation and in technical writing we

use the word "Christianity" to denote the particular system of belief, ritual practice, and sociological characteristics of the religion that grew up around Jesus Christ in various historical contexts. When we speak of Early Christianity we mean that system in its first two or three centuries; when we speak of Western Christianity we mean that system as it developed with Rome rather than Constantinople as its center; when we speak of Black Christianity we refer to that system as it predominated in African and Afro-American rather than European or Euro-American communities. In the first instance we focus upon the system of religion from the perspective of time; in the second, from the perspective of geography; and in the third, from the perspective of race and/or ethnicity. In none of these contexts can we refer to the Bible as the primary source of our information. We may consult Scripture about the particular features of the church in, say, the late first century A.D., but what we learn there will tell us very little about *Christianity*— in its social or cultural sense—in the Middle Ages, in Puritan New England, or among Negroes in the United States at the beginning of the Civil War. Let us not ask the Bible to do what it is not intended to do.

A Social and Cultural Fact of Life

It makes little sense, therefore, to say that "there is no such thing as Black Christianity," or that because the term cannot be found in Scripture we have no right to use it. Jesus Christ is the same yesterday, today, and forever (Heb. 13:8), but the way the religion about him has developed in different times, in various parts of the world, and among diverse races and nationalities is a cultural (anthropological) and societal (socio-logical) fact which nothing in Scripture would deny as having meaning worth our consideration. We may *say* that we are only interested in some pure form of Christianity that takes no account of these things, but we would find it impossible to describe without certain social and cultural presuppositions sticking to our description. We may as well be honest about it. Both the sins and the virtues of humankind are revealed in any study of Christianity, and we need not be so coy about why and how it developed among Black people as to reject out of hand the idea of a Black Christianity among other forms of the religion. Nor do we have any reason to suppose that the Holy Spirit has not been able to use that particular form to "win persons to Jesus Christ." Paul wrote: "I have become all things to all men, that I might by all means save some. I do it all for the sake of the gospel, that I may share in its blessings" (I Cor. 9:22–23).

To speak of a Black Christianity is simply to refer to a social and cultural fact of life. It just happens to be a fact that for the more than four hundred years of Black history in the New World, eighty-five to ninety percent of all Black Christians have worshiped with people of their own race in all-Black congregations. As we might expect, certain realities and characteristics of faith and life are attached to that simple fact. To recognize them and take them seriously in a discussion about the Christian religion is neither to condemn nor to commend it. It may be that we shall have something to say on both sides, but that comes later. At the moment, we only want to establish the realism of the terminology we are using. Whether we like it or not, there *is* such a thing as Black Christianity and it is neither unbiblical nor unchristian to acknowledge its existence.

In the short space of this book we cannot give an adequate summary of the history of Black Christianity in the United States, much less in Canada, the Caribbean, Central and South America, and Africa! Black religion, as such, has existed in all of these places for hundreds of years—sometimes as Christianity, sometimes in other forms antagonistic to Christianity, sometimes as a mixture of Christianity and some other religion, for example, neo-African cults and sects. The list of books at the back of this book suggests some references that will help to shed more light on the history and characteristics of what we may call Afro-American religion in the western hemisphere. Here, we must make suffice a brief sketch of the history of Black Christian churches of the United States, and then go on to more important considerations for answering the question, What is Black Christianity?

The Christianization of the African in America

At first the English settlers in the North American colonies had no intention of making Christians of their slaves. Not only was that considered dangerous, for a baptized slave might get the idea that freedom in Christ meant freedom in the civil order as well, but it was also considered unreasonable. The African slaves, who started to become numerous after 1619, were regarded as chattel—things—little more than uncivilized savages who would scarcely understand the Christian religion enough to be benefited by it.

There were, however, always some white people who disagreed. The Bishops of London, prelates of the Anglican Church, felt some missionary responsibility for the slaves and instructed priests of the Church of England in the colonies to minister to them. The Society of Friends, or Quakers, tried to give them some religious instruction. Beginning with Rev. Samuel Davies in Virginia, the Presbyterians showed some interest. By 1757 Davies reported that he had baptized at least one hundred and fifty Negroes, after preaching to them for about eighteen months. Other denominations received a few Black converts, slave as well as free, but none in any systematic way.

The major credit must go to the Separatist Baptists—rough-hewn, evangelistically-minded frontier preachers who built churches in the plantation country of Georgia and the Carolinas—and a new group called "Methodist societies" that broke away from the Anglicans after the Revolutionary War. These two American denominations, the Baptists and the Methodists, made the most consistent effort and had the greatest success in Christianizing the Africans in North America. After 1750 they were attracting slaves to their services in increasing numbers—much to the displeasure of most of the slaveowners.

Scholars are now more confident than they were a few years ago that the first slaves to become Christians, and many who followed them, held on to certain features of their old African beliefs. In Africa they had already recognized the existence of a supreme or high God. They had also practiced a form of water baptism and believed in the power of prayer. It is clear, therefore, that certain aspects of Christian belief and practice were not difficult for them to accept. And where they adopted new ideas and practices that were similar to the old ones, the African forms were strengthened rather than weakened, although they gradually were transformed. But the Africanized Christianity that was to flourish on the southern plantations, sometimes to the disgust and dismay of the white missionaries, included some features that had not been familiar to white believers, at least not in the same form. For example, there was much dancing and singing in the African style of "call and response," drumming—whenever permitted, for the masters were afraid drums could signal revolt—elaborate nighttime funeral customs, spirit possession (or what later Blacks were to call "getting happy"), conversion experiences involving flying, traveling great distances, or having an encounter with spirit guides in visions and dreams, and other African religious customs. Bishop Daniel A. Payne of the African Methodist Episcopal Church found that the ring shout, an unmistakable retention from the African past, was still being practiced in urban AME churches well into the nineteenth century.

Black Christianity continued to manifest African features, particularly after the whites granted Black preachers the freedom to organize "independent" Black congregations. The African Baptist or Bluestone Church appeared in 1758 near what is now Mecklenburg, Virginia. In 1773 David George and George Lisle were slave preachers of a Baptist congregation at Silver Bluff, South Carolina, across the river from Augusta, Georgia. This church was later relocated in Savannah and became the mother church for several others in the area. A flourishing congregation was organized in Williamsburg, Virginia, as early as 1776.

In the North, Black Methodist and Episcopal churches were founded by Richard Allen and Absalom Jones respectively in Philadelphia in 1794. The African Methodists split from the white church three years before and were quickly followed by Black members of white congregations in Baltimore, New York City, Wilmington, Charleston, and several other cities. A fever for independent churches, exempt from white supervision, was abroad in the free Black communities of the North. Such freedom was, of course, violently repressed in the South for many years. In the North most Black Christians were members of all-Black churches under the leadership of ministers of their own color long before the Civil War. But Black Christianity was not absent from the South, by any means. The slaves continued to worship with their masters in segregated pews, but many unordained preachers carried on an "invisible church" and were ready to claim their people as soon as emancipation was effected.

The Church of the Oppressed

From the beginning the Black Church was obsessed with a desire for the emancipation of the slaves. The African Methodists began with a revolt against white religious control which could not obscure their intentions with respect to the civil order as well. Three of the four earliest Black Baptist preachers we know much about—David George, George Lisle, and Amos Williams—fled slavery and founded new congregations in Nova Scotia, Jamaica, and the Bahamas. In its basic theology as well as its style, Black religion was a religion of freedom and the church was the core of the secular as well as religious movement to bring about the total abolition of slavery.

After the Civil War and throughout the Reconstruction period the churches led in the struggle to complete the work of emancipation from which both the North and the South were speedily retreating. Many Black preachers went into politics in the states of the former Confederacy and many were involved in the Freedmen's agencies during Reconstruction. The three great concerns of the churches during the remainder of the century were missions to the former slaves, education—particularly the type introduced by Booker T. Washington at Tuskegee Institute—and African missions, including selective emigration to Africa, as promoted by clergy such as the AME bishop Henry McNeal Turner and the Presbyterian educator Edward Wilmot Blyden.

In no other period of American history did the masses of Blacks need the church more desperately than between the turn of the century and the Great Depression. Whatever civil rights they thought they had won by the war had eroded by 1914. Indeed, Blacks were more segregated and discriminated against by the time of the First World War than they were in 1850. Racism was rife in all sections of the nation. In the South and border states the Ku Klux Klan and other anti-Negro hate groups were involved in an unprecedented wave of lynchings and race riots. One of the greatest migrations of the western hemisphere brought almost three million former agricultural workers and tenant farmers from the rural South into the cities between 1890 and 1929. The churches braced themselves to receive them and were finally overwhelmed by the demand for social services for people who often arrived at the railroad stations in Baltimore, Chicago, or Detroit with all their earthly possessions in burlap sacks.

During the Depression the churches were under severe pressure from new sects and cults which sprang up in the ghettos to feed the psychological hungers which the mainline denominations seemed powerless to satisfy. In the case of quasi-secular movements such as Father Divine's Peace Mission, Bishop Grace's House of Prayer for All People, the Moorish Science Temples, and Marcus Garvey's Universal Negro Improvement Association, economic and political as well as spiritual needs were met. And riding upon the crest of the concentric waves of Black Pentecostalism that flowed from Los Angeles in 1905, both the jazzy storefront churches and the hard-eyed cultic movements attracted more of the poor than the institutional churches.

Whether storefront or renovated Gothic cathedral, the church of the masses was a church of an oppressed group. In every city there were a few congregations that tried to meet the material needs of the migrants and projected an image of racial self-help and Black pride. They remained an important base for politicization when organizations like the National Association for the Advancement of Colored People (NAACP) slowly took over the leadership of the masses. But Black Christians were to see a steady diminution of the power of their preachers between the wars, and the influence of mainline religious institutions collapsed before an unremitting onslaught of secularism and anticlericalism in the Black urban community.

By the end of the Second World War many observers of the scene had pronounced the churches less than useful in the upward climb of the Negro from poverty and second-class citizenship. That judgment was probably too harsh, but there is no question but that the churches fell on bad days. Black clergy were said to be good for only two things: "preaching hellfire and raising money." Sociologist E. Franklin Frazier wrote that the church, more than any other institution, was responsible for the "backwardness" of the race.

The Era of Dr. King

It was at this lowest point of its influence that the churches were jolted into a new maturity by the refusal of an AME laywoman, Mrs. Rosa Parks, to sit in the segregated section of a city bus in Montgomery, Alabama. Led by a young Baptist preacher named Martin Luther King, Jr., the Montgomery bus boycott of 1955 demonstrated that, mobilized, organized, and inspired by their traditional religious leaders, Blacks were capable of exercising economic and political muscle against the power structure of the South. The movement caught on not only in the South but all over the nation. At one point in the early 1960s there were sixty local groups, led by clergy and affiliated with King's Southern Christian Leadership Conference, carrying on nonviolent direct action in support of the rights of Black people.

Out of that popular movement which began in Alabama came the widespread civil disorders of the North in the mid-1960s and the Black Power movement of 1965. The churches were deeply implicated in what happened. Dr. King and other Black church leaders dissociated themselves from the call for Black Power. But others—particularly in the northern cities—supported the young revolutionaries in their objective of Black self-determination without condoning what in some cities was nothing more than anarchy and the willful destruction of property. On the heels of the northern city rebellions of 1964–1967 the National Conference of Black Churchmen, a group of Black Power oriented church activists, moved Black Christians from a moderate social Christianity in the direction of Black theology, political radicalism, and Pan-Africanism. Although he may not have intended to do so, Dr. King had created a new Black consciousness in the churches.

It was in connection with this new consciousness and the upheavals of the late 1960s that the Black caucuses of the predominantly white denominations became most active in the struggle. Among them was a group called Black Presbyterians United. But we must interrupt our historical synopsis at this point in order to examine more closely the meaning of the religious impulses that emanate from Black Christianity and help us to understand what it is. We have looked quickly at the history of the churches, but what has been the intrinsic meaning of all this activity? What kind of Christianity was the Afro-American community evolving? That is the question to which we must turn to uncover the secret of Black religion in America.

Survival and Liberation

From the beginning of the African slave trade to the Civil War two identifiable motifs or themes developed side by side in the religion of Afro-Americans. We may call the oldest one the survival tradition, and the later one the liberation tradition. They represent two different kinds of religious sensibilities in the Black community.

The survival tradition arose primarily among the slaves as an antidote to their suffering and an expression of their dogged refusal to resign totally their humanity in the face of dehumanization. It is reflected in the reports of white missionaries which speak of the exoticism of the slaves' religious behavior—their love of conjuration, magic, voodoo and hoodoo (or more properly vodun and obeah, corruptions of the religions of West Africa). Rev. Charles C. Jones, the missionary responsible for the spread of Presbyterianism among the slaves in Georgia, referred to these interests among them as "various perversions of the Gospel" and, in terms of the obstacles they presented to the missionary, compared them to the product of "cultivated minds . . . of critics and philosophers." In other words, these Africans knew what they were doing. They threw up a bulwark of faith against a dehumanizing experience cloaked in the sanctimonious pretensions of their oppressors. They were trying to survive the Christian brainwashing that was an obvious accompaniment of their physical bondage.

The liberation tradition, on the other hand, grew out of the free Black community of the North. It reflected a psychologically more tolerable situation. Its emphasis was on personal and social elevation, moral behavior, and political liberty rather than on sheer survival. Perhaps a classic statement of the liberation tradition is what Bishop R. R. Wright gave as the founding principles of African Methodism: "Among other things, to exemplify in the black man the power of self-reliance, self-help by the exercise of free religious thought with executive efficiency."

The survival tradition was, we might say, the closest approximation to the African heritage. It was rural, lower class, and pragmatic. The liberation tradition was more urbane, more attuned to the influences of "respectable white Christians," and more idealistic. It became the tradition of the aspiring middle-class mulatto. Both traditions were, of course, interested in freedom. But the survival tradition sought whatever was available to it as interior freedom in emotional displays and in the prayer bands and ring shouts which proper Black ecclesiastics like Rev. John Chavis, Presbyterian, and Bishop Payne, AME, deplored. The liberation tradition, as far as possible, sought exterior freedom. It was inspired by the ideals of the American Revolution and white friends like the Quaker Anthony Benezet, or the Presbyterian Dr. Benjamin Rush, both of Philadelphia. Its concern was not so much coping, staying alive and sane under the brutality of the system, as proving the dignity and equality of Blacks who wanted to demonstrate, among other things, that they could own and operate a church just as well as white people.

W. E. B. Du Bois was the first to recognize these two strands of Black religion, although he does not give them the names we are using here. In *The Souls of Black Folk* he speaks of a religion that "became darker and more intense," that included a note of revenge, that was pessimistic and a "complaint and a curse, a wail rather than a hope, a sneer rather than a faith." The motif here is one of survival. He also speaks of a religion that is shrewd and optimistic, not above compromise and hypocrisy, but endeavoring "to turn the white man's weakness into the black man's strength." The motif is one of liberation. One does not have to accept the explicit descriptions Du Bois gives of these two traditions, but he seems to have discovered two different strands of faith in essential agreement with our analysis.

After emancipation the relationship between these seminal forms of religion become extremely complex and we need not get bogged down in a long discussion of that complexity. In one sense they continue to be identified in the difference the late E. Franklin Frazier made between the "invisible institution" of the church in the South and the "visible institution" in the North. But after the Civil War there is another sense in which the liberation tradition (modified by the sterner religiosity of the rural folk) came to dominate what had been the tradition of the masses of Negroes—a religion of internal freedom, which sneered at white religious hypocrisy, preserved a certain influence of African spirituality, and fought against the total destruction of the human personality which slavery perpetrated. The mainline Black churches, including the Presbyterian, successfully absorbed and domesticated this tradition, so that Black Christianity looked very much like white Christianity by the beginning of the twentieth century.

But the earlier survival tradition was never completely wiped out. The conditions of Black life were too precarious for that to happen. The survival tradition, more sophisticated than it was when William Wells Brown became acquainted with Dinkie, the hoodoo man, or the AMEs railed against "cornfield ditties" in their churches, nevertheless stirred restively in the bowels of the mainline Black Church. It was to break out most vociferously in Black Holiness and Pentecostalism and in the urban sects and cults, but Garveyism was the best example of the survival motif institutionalized. After that we can trace the development of survivalism from the 1920s, intricately intertwined with the liberation motif, through the period of civil rights to what Vincent Harding called "the religion of Black Power."

The main contribution of the sects and cults was that they revitalized and redirected the survival tradition of the folk by breaking through the restraints that were beginning to keep

Black religion firmly in the grip of the mainline tradition after the first quarter of the twentieth century. They opened old doors and broke through new ones which allowed certain forms of African, Asian, and Judaic spirituality to infuse Negro Christianity. Some of this creativity and openness to unfamiliar religious ideas filtered into the mainline churches, and while the liberation tradition continued to dominate their interpretation of the faith, they were never able to be as doctrinally pure as Payne and others would have wished.

This means that a considerable part of the Black Christian experience, particularly in the mass churches, has diverged from the theological and liturgical mainstream of the white church. It should not come as a surprise to anyone. Black Christianity had to wrestle with questions and come up with answers with which white Christianity, generally speaking, has had no commerce. It was the religion of a poor, oppressed class of people who were scarcely regarded as human beings by the rest of the society until the twentieth century. Moreover, it was a religion which, in certain important respects, veered from the main tradition because its roots were in sub-Saharan Africa rather than Europe. And although much of that inheritance had evaporated in African Methodism and the churches belonging to the predominantly white denominations, enough of it was still clinging to the lower end of the socioeconomic spectrum by the beginning of this century to give a certain flavor to the religion of the masses. It is for this reason that some people could call that genre of Christianity "Black" in the 1960s and instinctively understand what was meant by the term without quite being able to explain it in words.

The Same, Yet Different

What is it—this indefinable quality of Christianity as practiced among Afro-American people? A certain lilt of music to which the body as well as the soul must respond? The way some choirs come down the aisle singing "We've Come This Far by Faith"—with that little half step that looks as if it might break out into a holy dance at any moment? The way the Bible is interpreted in colorful word pictures as the preacher "tells the story"? The way the Holy Spirit can fall upon the congregation and have folks laughing and crying at the same time, waving their arms in the air and calling out their "Amens" and "Thank you, Jesus"? The traditional counterclockwise promenade to the offering table? The deacons' devotional period of "lining hymns" before the regular service begins? The rich poetry of the spirituals and all the talk about "going home" and "glory land" in the contemporary gospel songs? On another, more cognitive, level of experience: Is it the persistent belief in direct communication with God and the belief that "He may not come when you want Him to, but He's always on time"? Is it an openness to doctrinal ideas that "feel right" to the community rather than conform to some canon of orthodoxy? Is it a willingness to use the church for winning elections as well as winning souls—an assumption that religion has to do with all of life—a refusal to define sharply a separation between the sacred and the profane, the religious and the secular?

All of these and other characteristics which we cannot go into give the traditional Black church a distinctive atmosphere and coloration that distinguishes it from the mainstream of both fundamentalism and Protestant evangelicalism. The church is still a primary expression of Black life and culture despite the fact that other institutions are now challenging its leadership. It is the last bastion of the ethnic particularity of the Afro-American community in the United States, combining in a variegated tapestry of older and newer beliefs, ideologies, mythologies, attenuated cultural symbols and social roles, perceptions of reality and patterns of behavior, those elements which add up to what it means to be Black—that indefinable quality of Black Christianity that is the same and yet so different from the standard brand of Christianity in America.

It goes without saying that every Black Christian is not aware of these differences and only a few could describe them, much less define them. But that should not surprise us. A person who has spent his or her entire life in the inner city—at least before the advent of television—would not be expected to believe that there was any other way of life. Even in the 1980s a relatively small number of Black church members know anything about the Sunday morning worship experience or the week-to-week life-style of a typical, middle-class white congregation—or vice versa. Even Black Presbyterians or Episcopalians continue to be marginal to those denominations, particularly on the congregational level, and might assume that what they believe and do is standard throughout the church. There is indeed little difference on the surface between these congregations and those of the same economic and social class in the white community. But given the traditional role of the Black church and the status of the preacher in the Black community, even the Black congregations of white denominations are likely to conform to a set of norms different from those of their sister congregations. They have a vague sense of being different even as they strive to be the same.

Finally—A Definition

Because we have been saying that Black Christianity contains essentially indefinable qualities, it would seem odd to venture a definition. But we have come to the end of this chapter and before going on to look at Black Presbyterianism as such, we ought to close our discussion with some definition that we can take with us into the next part of our study.

Let us be clear about one thing. The usefulness of definitions is not that they settle matters once and for all, but that they give us some starting point in trying to understand reality.

What follows below is not the end of the study of Black Christianity but the beginning. Our definition is a tentative, experimental model that will, we hope, lend itself to further reflection and research. As we proceed to study the phenomenon we are calling Black Christianity we should, from this point, begin to improve upon our definition and make it more accurate and more serviceable to our purpose. At the end, we should know better what we are talking about when we use the term.

The term "Black Christianity" is sometimes used to refer to the Christian religion as practiced by all peoples of African descent—whether in Africa or in the Diaspora. Here we have been using the term more precisely as referring to the Afro-American or Black community in North America. *Thus, Black Christianity is that particular appropriation which Afro-Americans made of the religion that was first delivered to them by white Americans.* It is the same, yet different from Christianity as practiced by most white people in that it continues to reflect, however partially and dimly, an African religious and cultural inheritance that was looked down upon by most white Christians.

But more clearly, Black Christianity reflects the historic struggle against racism and oppression that Black people have experienced and attempted to understand through the gospel of Jesus Christ. The determination to be free, therefore, is at its core and is expressed in many ways—in music, modes of worship, styles of preaching and prayer, ethical commitments and ideas about social justice, and in what many Black Christians believe about God and the immediacy of his relationship to his creation. Black Christianity is characterized on the one hand, by a deep spirituality—highly personal and emotional—and on the other, by a hardheaded, pragmatic approach to reality that is strongly communal and political in its orientation.

Black Christianity is most pronounced today in the churches of the masses which are affiliated with Black denominations, but it is also found, with increasing frequency, in Black congregations within the predominantly white denominations.

Let us now ask what this Black Christianity looks like in one particular constituency of a predominantly white church— that is to say, among Black Presbyterians. In so doing we will be examining a particular strain of Presbyterian tradition with which Inez Jones had no acqaintance. It may well be that this is why she felt so estranged and useless in the predominantly white institution in which she found herself.

3
Black People and Presbyterianism

Psalm 68:31
Acts 10:1–35
Ephesians 2:11–22

If we had difficulty defining Black Christianity, we will have even greater problems defining Black Presbyterianism. With all that has been said about Blackness—its orientation to the African cultural endowment, its candid emotionality, its pragmatic spirituality, and its concern about freedom from racism and other forms of oppression—nothing would seem more unlikely than to find it in combination with the cold, unornamented, duty-bound religion of Presbyterianism. On the other hand, that allegation cannot be taken at face value because the Reformed or Presbyterian tradition was much concerned about freedom from unauthorized civil power and legitimate resistance to religious oppression. Perhaps that was one of the reasons why, throughout the history of the Presbyterian churches in North America, true Calvinists had a bad conscience about white racism and always found it difficult to shrug off a sense of responsibility for racial justice. Yet we would have to admit that, taken as a whole, Anglo-Saxon Presbyterianism is about as close to the Black religious and cultural tradition as "Annie Laurie" by the Royal Bagpipes is to "Body and Soul" by the Modern Jazz Quartet.

Whatever can be said assuredly about Black people and the Presbyterian Church it cannot be said that they come together naturally. Not only did some Black folks in Hattiesburg, Mississippi, have difficulty even pronouncing the word "Presbyterian" during the civil rights marches, but they found it rather incredible that some Black people in the North called themselves Presbyterian. They had not known of any Black Presbyterians, and judging from what they observed about white Presbyterians, would not expect to find any who were Black. And Inez Jones's mother would have found considerable support among most of her friends and neighbors for her contention that when you meet a Black person who has become a Presbyterian, somebody has probably been tampering with his or her religion.

Well, most of the time—but not always! In the Carolinas and Georgia there are Black families whose connections with the Presbyterian Church go back six generations, and the First African Presbyterian Church in Philadelphia has had a continuous existence for one hundred and seventy-five years. For a long time there have been people who could only be described as Afro-Saxon Presbyterians who were proud of the fact that "Lift Ev'ry Voice and Sing" and Paul Laurence Dunbar's poems were no more familiar to them than the Shorter Catechism and the Westminster Confession. The names of Lucy Craft Laney, a slave who founded a pioneering Black school and whose father was a Southern Presbyterian minister after the Civil War, Daniel Jackson Sanders, a former slave who became the first Black president of Biddle University (now Johnson C. Smith University), and Albert Byron McCoy, for many years the director of Sunday school missions in the North Carolina heartland of Black Presbyterianism, remind us that there have been Black people who had not the least doubt that their calling into Presbyterianism was just as natural as that of any Scotch-Irish family in Richmond or Pittsburgh. They were proper Presbyterians in every sense of the word and would have been offended by the suggestion that they might have been anything else.

These considerations, however, take nothing away from the fact that Presbyterianism, as it was transplanted to North America from Great Britain, was at a severe disadvantage compared to the Baptist and Methodist denominations in appealing to Black people and taking sides with them against slavery in the eighteenth and nineteenth centuries. But before we get into a rapid survey of this history let us locate the Presbyterian churches in the history of Western Christianity for the sake of beginning at the beginning.

A System of Church Government

Presbyterians believe that their form of the church goes back to New Testament days when the apostles installed in each church a group of officials who ruled, called presbyters, or "elders," and a second group who performed acts of service and charity, called deacons (Acts 14:23; Titus 1:5; and Acts 6:1–6, although the term "deacon" is not used). According to this practice the pastor was nothing more nor less than an elder who had been given teaching rather than explicitly ruling responsibilities and was the person entrusted with the administration of the Word and Sacraments.

The sixteenth-century Protestant Reformation in Europe brought this Biblical practice to remembrance when the Reformers turned to the Scriptures as the sole authority for how the church should be governed. A Presbyterian form of church government was first introduced in Geneva, Switzerland, by John Calvin (1509–1564) and spread to other Reformed churches throughout Europe. By the middle of the sixteenth century all educated whites knew that there were Black men and women in West Africa and that they were being enslaved by Christians for a lifetime of hard labor in the Spanish West Indies and Latin America. Yet one searches in vain to find where the great Reformers took notice that the renunciation of man-stealing was the expected morality of any pious Protestant. It is interesting, in this regard, that John Knox (c. 1514–1572), a Scottish Reformer who is the second great figure of Presbyterian history, said of Calvin's Geneva that it was "the most perfect school of Christ that ever was in earth since the days of the apostles."

Presbyterians could be greatly exercised about church government, but it took more than two hundred years from the days of Calvin and Knox for a judicatory of a Presbyterian church to take up the matter of African slavery. During the years in between and for almost another century afterward Presbyterians held slaves without any authoritative body of church law or doctrine to tell them that they were committing a sin. The Methodists were not to appear until the middle of the eighteenth century, but under their leaders, John Wesley and Thomas Coke, they did much better for the cause of racial justice. Early Methodists in the West Indies and the North American colony may have held slaves, but they knew that their "society" and many of their preachers were opposed to it on theological and ethical grounds.

Calvinism is commonly associated with Presbyterianism and refers to more than a system of church government. It is essentially a system of theology that emphasizes the sovereignty and glory of God as the ground of all religious, social, cultural, and political life and calls the believer to total dependence upon God's will over all things. The doctrine of predestination is often mentioned as the keystone of Reformed or Presbyterian theology, although it has several times been modified from its original severity by most modern Presbyterian denominations. But as important as theology is to Presbyterians it would be correct to say that today Presbyterianism refers more to a distinctive form of government—church rule at local, regional, and national levels by pastors and ruling elders rather than by bishops or other overseers—than to a world view or plan of salvation.

We do not intend to enter here upon a thorough discussion of the doctrinal basis of Calvinism and Presbyterianism, but a few more words are in order to help us set Presbyterianism in its historical context prior to the conversion of African slaves in the American colonies of the eighteenth century.

Puritanism, Presbyterianism, and Revolution

During the sixteenth century Henry VIII succeeded in establishing in England what was essentially a Roman Catholic Church independent of Rome. The Church of England refused to recognize the pope, but it left many of the rites and doctrines of standard Roman Catholicism intact. By the time Elizabeth took the throne in 1558 many people had been won to the model of a theocratic state, that "most perfect school of Christ" which Calvin had created in Geneva, and sought to purify the Church of England by discarding all Roman Catholic practices and returning to what they believed were the characteristics of the New Testament church. Among these "Puritans" were Presbyterians. They formed the first English presbytery in 1572 and refused to conform to Elizabeth's idea of Anglicanism. They were, however, less radical than their fellow Puritans who were called Congregationalists or Independents because they wanted a reformed Church of England in which every local church was independent.

After Elizabeth's death in 1603, Presbyterian Puritans continued to be persecuted by James VI of Scotland, who succeeded her as James I of England. The obsession of Puritanism for a culture, church, and state totally anti-Catholic and governed by the pure morality of the Bible led inevitably to revolution. Throughout this period Presbyterians had nothing to say about slavery in the English colonies of the New World, but a great deal to say about what vestments clergy should wear and what liturgy should be used in divine worship. Charles I, who succeeded his father, James I, was not disposed to tolerate their dissent and harried the Puritans, including Presbyterians, out of England to the wilds of North America. For his pains he was executed in 1649 after civil war raged in his kingdom for seven years. During this period

Presbyterianism was planted in the New World by colonists who emigrated to New England and founded the Massachusetts Bay Colony in 1630. The doctrines of Puritanism were systematized and promulgated in England by the Westminster Assembly of ministers and laymen which met from 1643 to 1649 by order of Parliament to make use of its advice on the final reformation of the Church of England.

What is called the Westminster Confession came to be the official creedal statement of Presbyterians and the most influential pronouncement of Protestant theology for American Christians in the seventeenth and eighteenth centuries. Not only was it authoritative for Presbyterians, but Congregationalists and many Baptists, with certain omissions and additions, adopted the Westminster Confession as the substance of doctrine taught by the Scriptures. The original Confession included thirty-three articles with proof texts bearing upon what has generally been recognized as the five points of Calvinism: divine sovereignty, human depravity, limited atonement, irresistible grace, and the perseverance of the saints. Today most Presbyterian churches hold to a more contemporary statement of faith, but one based upon the Westminster Confession. It was the intention of the Westminster divines that Presbyterianism would become the official form of government for the Church of England, but Oliver Cromwell, the dangerously self-righteous leader of the civil war, opposed Presbyterianism. Congregationalism—holding that neither bishop nor presbytery had the authority to discipline a congregation—became the order of the day. Presbyterianism, therefore, never gained a firm foothold in England and indeed was contested by Congregationalism and other forms of dissent in New England.

It was, nevertheless, strong enough in Scotland and Wales, and through immigration to the New World, Presbyterians were to see their version of the Christian faith become one of the most powerful expressions of Protestantism in the world. American Presbyterians organized their first presbytery in 1706 and were among the most enthusiastic supporters of the revolt against England in 1776. The representative form of government adopted by the Continental Congress was greatly influenced by the Presbyterian form of church government. The high educational standards of Presbyterian clergy and the explicit ideas they had about secular morality contributed to the dominant role the Presbyterian Church played throughout the period of the Revolutionary War and into the nineteenth century.

How Presbyterians Related to Blacks

It is at the point of the period leading up to the Revolution of 1776, known by some in those days as the "Presbyterian rebellion," that we pick up the emergent relationship between the Presbyterians and the Black, mainly slave, population of colonial America. According to Rev. W. H. Franklin, a Black Presbyterian educator who wrote *The Early History of the Presbyterian Church in the U.S.A. Among the Negroes*, an undated pamphlet in the Presbyterian Historical Society, the first Blacks were introduced to Presbyterianism as slaves working in the homes of pious white Presbyterians. They were taught to read and to memorize passages from the Shorter Catechism and the Bible. During the eighteenth and nineteenth centuries many white people believed that the words of Ps. 68:31 were being fulfilled—Black people of the world were being converted to Christianity and masters should do what they could to promote the salvation of their "Ethiopians." Franklin writes that they began with children. Black children were often taught in the home by white children or other members of the family.

> They attended many Sabbath schools with the white people and were taught at the same time and place or in the afternoon. If the colored children had their Sabbath school in the afternoon, they were taught by the white members of the

church. This is why the slaves and servants coming from Presbyterian homes showed superior intelligence.

The first organized Presbyterian effort to reach the slaves was initiated by Rev. Samuel Davies, a New Side (or revivalistic, modified Calvinist) Presbyterian minister, in 1747. Davies preached in Virginia, and out of his labors developed the Hanover Presbytery, which included all Presbyterian churches south of the Potomac. Ten years later Davies reported that he had baptized some one hundred and fifty slaves and commented further on his belief that the care of the souls of Black slaves was an "awful and important trust" from God. It was not until 1789 that the first General Assembly was held and the topic of slavery began to be debated in the highest judicatory of the Presbyterian Church. Although a few colonial ministers and laymen openly opposed slavery during the eighteenth century, the Presbyterian Church as a whole, with its strong southern constituency in the Carolinas, put its emphasis on the religious instruction of the slaves rather than their emancipation. The hard fact is that Presbyterians were more prejudiced against Blacks than either the Methodists or the Baptists. No white church did very much, but both of those denominations made a bolder effort than did the Presbyterians to rid themselves of slaveholders and to bring slave converts into their congregations. Part of the consequence was that both churches were regarded more favorably by Blacks and attracted a larger number of slaves than did the Presbyterians.

There was an aristocratic elitism about the racism of many Presbyterian clergy. At a meeting of the Synod of Virginia on November 9, 1867, Rev. Robert L. Dabney, arguing against the ecclesiastical equality of Black Presbyterian preachers in the Southern Church, made a statement that illustrates the prejudice and self-delusion of white Presbyterians on the race question.

I oppose the entrusting of the destinies of our Church, in any degree whatsoever, to black rulers, because that race is not

trustworthy for such position. There may be *a few exceptions:*
(I do not believe I have ever seen one, though I have known
Negroes whom I both respected and loved, in their proper
position) but I ask emphatically: Do legislatures frame general
laws to meet the rare exceptions? or do they adjust them to the
general average?

All Black Presbyterian ministers and commissioners experienced discrimination at meetings of presbyteries, and bitterly
complained about it. A Black minister of the Northern
Church, Rev. Samuel Cornish, wrote in *The Colored American* for March 11, 1837:

> I have seen a minister of Jesus Christ sitting in Presbytery, with
> his white brethren in the ministry, who, though it had been
> announced that full provision was made among the church
> members for every brother . . . yet [was] left by himself in the
> church for three successive days, without dinner or tea,
> because no Christian family could be found in the congrega-
> tion, who would admit him to their table, on account of his
> color.

Perhaps the best evidence of the racism of the Presbyterians
was the church's attitude toward slavery during the early years
of the nineteenth century. No church was more high-sound-
ing and profound in its Biblical and theological analysis of
slavery and did less about it. The issue first came up in a
Presbyterian judicatory in 1774. From that year until the Civil
War divided the denomination in 1861, only a handful of
embattled white Presbyterians dared to challenge the church
to face up to the toleration of slaveholding. Consider, for
example, the action of the Presbytery of Transylvania in 1797.
The question was put to the presbytery: "Is slavery a moral
evil?" The vote gave the answer as "Yes." A second question
was put: "Are all persons who hold slaves guilty of a moral
evil?" The answer given was "No." When a third question
attempted to get the presbytery to decide, if not all slaveholders, which of them should be considered guilty of a moral evil,

the answer was: "Resolved that the question . . . be put off until a future day." The Presbyterian historian Andrew E. Murray remarks dryly: "This day seems never to have arrived."

The case of Rev. George Bourne, of Lexington Presbytery in Virginia, is an infamous example of Presbyterian pharisaism on the slavery question. Bourne had been deposed by his presbytery for strong antislavery views. The Virginia slaveholders obviously manufactured a case against him and the matter was brought before the General Assembly of 1818, where the deposition was upheld at the same time that the Assembly issued a resounding antislavery pronouncement. Bourne accused Presbyterians of rank hypocrisy. The antislavery pronouncement which many southerners voted for, he argued, was simply to satisfy the consciences of the northern and eastern churches in exchange for their permitting the slaveholders of Virginia to have their way in unfrocking him as a dangerous enemy of their slave system. "They only intended by it," Bourne said of the General Assembly's northern commissioners, "to blind their eyes to the true character and wickedness of slavery, and to silence their outcry and disquietude respecting their being participants with their [the slaveholders] guilt."

Black Presbyterians must have watched this spectacle of their church's pious fraud with little humor. It was becoming increasingly clear to them that the Presbyterian Church condemned slavery in theory and condoned it in practice. Ironically, the preaching and teaching ministry to Black people increased in inverse proportion to the church's commitment to radical abolitionism. The more white Presbyterians tiptoed around the outright repudiation of slaveholding Christians, the more their consciences drove them to the next best thing—bringing the poor slaves to Jesus and preparing them for membership in the Presbyterian Church by religious instruction. In other words, "doing good for poor Black folk" easily became an acceptable substitute for emancipating them.

Certainly few white Christians in the nineteenth century

were able to "do good" better than the Presbyterians. They were the backbone of the growing middle and upper classes in most of the areas where Blacks were numerous. The Presbyterian pastors and missionaries were the best educated in the nation and, therefore, could be of the greatest assistance to Black people who were always looking for opportunities to learn how to read and write. In terms of educational opportunities the Presbyterian churches were much superior to the more zealous but less erudite Baptist and Methodist churches. If we must have a reason why some Blacks were drawn to the Presbyterian Church, despite its elitism and in the face of its hypocrisy on the question of slavery, the answer probably lies in the widely publicized opportunities the Presbyterians gave them to improve themselves through reading, writing, arithmetic, manners, morals, and better social contacts. Presbyterians placed an uncommon emphasis on these things, and no doubt the denomination's greatest contribution to both slaves and freed Blacks was advancement in learning and the proprieties of the upper classes.

The First African Presbyterian Church of Philadelphia prided itself in sponsoring a day school that was strongly supported by white Presbyterians. It is not surprising that in this church, according to one of its early pastors, "the claims of the Gospel . . . [were] addressed more to the conviction of the conscience and understanding of the people, than to the prejudices and passions." Presbyterians believed in an educated ministry and laity. The Synod of New York and New Jersey established an African School in 1816 which continued with some difficulty for nine years. The earliest Black Presbyterian missionary, John Chavis, organized a school for both whites and Blacks in North Carolina, despite laws throughout the South after 1831 that prohibited anyone from teaching slaves to read and write. Almost all Black Presbyterian pastors augmented their salaries by teaching. Relatively few Blacks in the North and only a small proportion of the estimated seventy thousand slaves owned by Presbyterians in the South answered the call to discipleship, but those who did may well have come into the church as much for educational and social advancement as for any other reason. It was well known that the soberminded followers of John Calvin put more stock in the enlightenment of the mind than in the emotional experiences of conversion which were stressed by the Methodists and Baptists.

We can, therefore, make the tentative conclusion that one of the reasons Blacks joined the Presbyterian Church and remained in it had to do with what they believed they were getting from it in terms of education and status. It must have occurred to some that both had limited value in view of the disabilities they still suffered. But what Black Presbyterians were prepared to do was to turn the intellectual weapons that whites put into their hands against racism in both the church and society. No Black ministers illustrate this strategy better during the antebellum period than the two New York Presbyterian clergymen Samuel Cornish and Theodore S. Wright. These men, together with Henry Highland Garnet, J. W. C. Pennington, Francis Grimke, and other clergymen who labored in the Presbyterian churches before the turn of the century, illustrate the true spirit of Black Presbyterianism—to use every resource of a trained mind and a gentle spirit to uplift the race, and to hold constantly before the eyes of the church and the conscience of the nation the mandate of liberty and justice for all.

Pioneers of Black Presbyterianism

Samuel Cornish is best known as the editor of the first Black newspaper, *Freedom's Journal*, but in 1822 he had the distinction of founding the First Colored Presbyterian Church of New York City, after laboring as a missionary to indigent Blacks in the slums of lower Manhattan. Theodore S. Wright was the first Black to graduate from a theological seminary— Princeton Seminary, 1828. He took over the New York

congregation after Cornish and made it the second largest
Black church in the city. These two men were close friends
and comrades-in-arms as far as prejudice and discrimination
were concerned. They stood side by side to represent the free
Black community in the antislavery movement of the 1820s
and 1830s, although Wright refused to leave the pastorate for
the abolitionist lecture circuit. Together they attacked the
segregated seating in Presbyterian churches and chided their
white brethren for so boldly denouncing slavery in the South,
while being unwilling to grant civil rights to Blacks in the
North. But neither of them limited his protest activities to the
integration of the lily-white structures of the Presbyterian
Church. Although he remained a Presbyterian to the end,
Cornish favored Blacks attending their own churches, lest
"they weaken the hands and discourage the hearts of their
ministers, by leaving them to preach to empty pews." It was
certainly not expected that whites would attend Black
churches. Neither Cornish nor Wright lowered his dignity by
currying the favor of prejudiced whites. In the 1840s Wright
broke with his moderate white friends by deliberately disobey-
ing the law against giving assistance to fugitive slaves. He
ignored the cries of reverse racism and the betrayal of white
allies in the struggle against racism to urge Blacks to close their
ranks, to organize politically and fight for the right to vote,
rather than continue to depend upon the eventual conversion
of whites by moral suasion.

These two crusading ministers, and fellow Black Presbyterian clergy like J. W. C. Pennington, Elymas P. Rogers, and
Henry Highland Garnet, were not willing to drop quietly out
of sight in the denomination, as many might have wished.
Instead, they sought to fulfill their ordination vows as teaching
elders by making the denomination face up to the gospel it
proclaimed. In so doing, they emboldened both races to take
increasingly more radical stances in the tumultuous years
leading up to the Civil War. Wright was the mentor and
inspirer of the famous Rev. Henry H. Garnet, whose powerful

address in 1843 called upon the slaves to begin an armed struggle. Garnet was a Presbyterian firebrand and there were few abolitionists, including the redoubtable Frederick Douglass, who could match his zeal for getting Black people to stand on their own feet and do something about the liberation of the millions of their brothers and sisters in the South.

Black Presbyterians have been criticized by other Blacks for remaining in a predominantly white church where they were under the double jeopardy of having to fight both class consciousness and racism. But it is possible that the reason these men were among the most militant of Black ministers was precisely the necessity of having to carry on a continuous struggle for their dignity and self-respect in a racist church that had little to do with the impoverished masses. It is also possible that their close association with whites in the church, their exposure to the best of white learning, and their determination to participate in the denomination as equals with whites and without excuses for shoddy work, gave them unusual self-confidence compared to many other Black clergy, and a more accurate understanding and assessment of the weaknesses of the white church and society. It very well may be that because of their involvement in the Presbyterian Church, they cultivated the knowledge and skill to play the adversary role against bigotry and injustice to the best effect. Ministers of the independent Black Baptist and Methodist churches gave outstanding leadership to the movement for abolition and civil rights prior to 1861, but none were more courageous and effective than the Black clergy of the Presbyterian Church.

The Mission to the Freedmen

The General Assembly, meeting in Pittsburgh on May 18, 1865, took action to dispatch missionaries, teachers, and material resources into the South in aid of the newly emancipated slaves. It proved to be a decision that was to have inestimable consequences for the ingathering and nurture of

Blacks by the Presbyterian Church. It is possible that most of what has been right about the church's involvement with Black people and most of what has been wrong about that involvement have a common matrix in the policies and strategies of the Freedmen's Board established at the end of the Civil War. Although the number of Blacks who actually joined the Presbyterian Church as a result of the missionary effort in the South was not impressive, the effect of the far-flung system of Presbyterian colleges and parochial schools upon the general quality of Black life was extraordinary. White missionaries braved social ostracism and even physical violence at the hands of white southerners as they ministered to the former slaves, many of whom were members of the Southern Presbyterian Church who refused to go back. The northerners gave themselves sacrificially to the organization of churches, schools, and community projects throughout the former Confederacy. The extent of the educational effort alone can be measured by the fact that as late as 1927 there were 19,000 Blacks enrolled in more than 160 Presbyterian schools and colleges.

On the other hand, one gets a sense of the paternalism of some of these whites in the statement of one of the field secretaries of the Freedmen's Board describing the work: "Need we say the face of that prostrate helpless man is black. The strong beautiful hand reaching out to him is white." Questionable presuppositions about what Blacks could and should learn, condescension about making them over into the image of white Presbyterians, and the unwillingness of the whites to surrender control of the institutions and programs to Black leadership, all conspired to create difficulties with which the church is still contending. Because of the inability of Blacks to fund their own work at adequate levels they had to depend upon the Freedmen's Board to pay salaries and provide other aid to the field. This not only created a feeling of dependency, which militated against good stewardship habits among the Blacks, but it also made it difficult for their presbyteries and synods to exercise ecclesiastical authority over the pastors and churches "on welfare" with the board.

As late as the 1940s Black Presbyterians were still faced with the problem of white control because of policies and practices begun by the Freedmen's Board. Clearly the board was not an unmixed blessing. In 1914 it even sought to supersede the Home Mission Board and take over work with Blacks in the North. This was staunchly opposed, but the all-white board continued to administer missions among Black Presbyterians in the North as well as in the South until 1923. A new Board of National Missions was then created by the church and within it the Division of Work with Colored Persons—albeit, under a white administrator. Blacks were to feel some sense of self-determination in the church by 1938 when Rev. Albert B. McCoy was elected the first Black to serve as secretary of the new unit responsible for work among the Black constituency. But even under the new dispensation some of the trappings of the old system remained, and in the South, where the main strength of Black Presbyterianism has always been, Blacks continued to protest that they were either neglected or obliged to suffer the high-handed treatment of the church well into the 1950s.

Black Presbyterian Solidarity

In the face of long-standing problems of racial equality with both the Northern and Southern branches of the Presbyterian Church it is not difficult to appreciate why Black Presbyterian ministers would have united for concerted action. In 1893 Grimke, Armstrong, Anderson, and Reeves—four distinguished pastors—founded the Afro-Presbyterian Council at the First African Church of Philadelphia. Actually there had been informal caucusing among Black clergy and laity even before the Civil War. The Afro-American Council proved to be necessary not only for political reasons but also to provide a more regular opportunity for the fellowship and mutual edification that was hard to come by in the "integrated" judicatories of the Northern Church, not to mention in the South, where a separate Black Presbyterian denomination was almost created. Now the Northern clergy had a formal organization that could represent the political, religious, and social interests of their constituents. In 1947 the name was changed to the Council of the North and West, for almost all Black Presbyterians in the South were members of Black presbyteries and synods and needed no racial caucus.

Occasion was given at the 1904 General Assembly to test the strength of the Afro-American Council. The Northern Presbyterians accepted an overture to seek union with the Cumberland Presbyterians, a church of southerners who would not countenance integration into interracial presbyteries with the Black congregations that happened to be within their bounds. The Blacks opposed such a union, but the Assembly adopted the overtures and created a Special Committee on the Territorial Limits of Presbyteries. In its report the committee recommended segregation, with the observation about Black people that "as a race they are inferior to the whites in culture, mental and moral development, and civilization; and for this reason they have a peculiar claim upon the stronger race for help and guidance." But in separate judicatories, of course.

Dr. Francis Grimke, pastor of the prestigious Fifteenth Street Church in the nation's capital, led the Council in that fight, but to no avail. The presbyteries approved the union and the affirmative vote the following year at the 1905 General Assembly settled the matter for years to come.

The Council of the North and West became virtually a Black jurisdiction within the white church. Blacks used it to empower the de facto separation that had been upheld by the 1905 decision and the insensitivity of the church to the needs of its Black members. It was the Supreme Court decision against "separate but equal" in 1954 that emboldened the denominations to a greater effort to desegregate and, in a burst of optimism about the future, the Council of the North and West went out of business in 1957 by turning its assets over to the General Assembly and declaring that its usefulness had come to an end in this era of good feeling.

The massive resistance to the Brown decision, and to the civil rights movement generally, proved the optimism to be premature. In 1964 Blacks began once again to caucus in what was called the Concerned Presbyterians group. Edler G. Hawkins, Robert P. Johnson, Bryant George, and other activist clergy pressed the denomination to support the work of Dr. King by creating, within the structure of the denomination, the Commission on Religion and Race in 1963. Five years later the call went out to renew the Black caucus at a national gathering in St. Louis. As one brochure put it: "The walls of segregation seemed as impregnable as ever, and there was little evidence that the church's practice was beginning to correspond with professions. There was much wrong in Zion!"

It was part of the strategy of the 1968 meeting which created Black Presbyterians United (BPU) to push the younger and more aggressive leaders into the forefront and for the older, more prestigious pastors and executives to line up behind them in key decision-making posts of the denomination. Accordingly, Rev. E. Wellington Butts became the first president of Black Presbyterians United. With youthful energy and un-compromising commitment to solidarity and self-development he led the new group in declaring:

> Black men and women must be enabled to significantly determine their lives and the nature of their communities. They must be free and able to respond to the forces that play upon their life. Black persons must have the opportunity to participate on an equal basis in all aspects of the larger pluralistic society and to work their will in the councils of nations and empires. To this end we seek power and for this purpose we bring this Black caucus into existence.

So it was that Blacks within the Presbyterian Church came of age in the 1960s after more than one hundred and fifty years of an uphill and downhill struggle within a church that continually had difficulty matching good intentions with performance and overcoming the natural conservatism of wealth and respectability. We have not attempted to relate the whole fascinating story of what Black Presbyterians did during that long ordeal, but only to trace the bare outline of their movement out of self-effacing innocence and gratitude for what they had received, to the realization of what they brought to the church, and the necessity of organizing to give that contribution greater visibility and penetration in the life of the denomination. Dr. Leland Stanford Cozart, the first Black president of Barber-Scotia College, wisely stated what had been the reality about Black people and Presbyterianism since the two came together in the eighteenth century.

> Because of the Presbyterian Church, the Negro in America today is infinitely the richer in body, mind and spirit; because of the Negro, the Presbyterian Church is immeasurably more responsive to human needs, more brotherly and more Christian.

But we must turn now to some of the weaknesses of Black Presbyterianism—weaknesses that sometimes grow out of a misuse and misunderstanding of God's blessings. There are surely temptations in being a part of a powerful, predominantly white denomination in a world full of misery and injustice. How do Black men and women discover who they really are under such circumstances, what their heritage is, and how God would use them to break down "the dividing wall of hostility" so that reconciliation can be the consequence of authentic liberation?

4
The Middle-Class Black Church and the Identity Crisis

Psalm 137:4
Esther 4:13–14
Luke 11:24–26

In 1964 Northern Presbyterianism descended upon Hattiesburg, Mississippi, when the Council on Church and Race, an agency of the General Assembly, set up an office and temporary dormitory in the Black community for Presbyterian ministers coming into town to assist the local civil rights groups. The volunteers from the North were mostly young, white clergy who had answered the Macedonian call that had gone out from the Student Nonviolent Coordinating Committee and other groups. They canvassed the Black neighborhoods for prospective voters, walked picket lines in protest of the refusal of white officials to register their prospects, taught in the emergency Freedom Schools, and in various other ways provided rural Mississippi with a Northern Presbyterian presence for several months. It was the Reconstruction period all over again.

The Black folks of the area in which the Hattiesburg Ministers' Project was located were overwhelmingly Baptist and various strains of Holiness. They were poor people and had little education. They and their ancestors had been the victims of the worst forms of southern racism for generations. Many of them who worked daily with the Presbyterian ministers were particularly curious about those ministers from the North who were Black.

"I seed some white Pedestrians downtown," said one lady who provided additional lodging for the project, "but hain't never heard tell of no *Black* Pedestrians."

When one of the ministers told her about the large number of Black Presbyterians who lived in the South and suggested that she should visit one of their churches sometime, she replied that although it wasn't her business, Black folks were supposed to be either Baptist or Methodist. "Ain't likely I'd be goin' to no Pedestrian church, Reverend. Ya'll prob'ly be too high class fo' po' folks like me."

The Myth of Exclusiveness

The lady in Hattiesburg did not know it, but she was voicing the opinion of many Black people about the Presbyterian Church—too high class for Black folks. The opinion is not limited to people in the slums of Hattiesburg, Mississippi. It was and is shared by many people today in Atlanta, Charlotte, Philadelphia, and Detroit. But is it true?

The question partly revolves around whether or not a Black Presbyterian church is "Black." Some people begin by denying the appropriateness of the term "Black church" for congregations of predominantly white denominations like the Presbyterians. They would argue that not only do Black Presbyterians reflect class attitudes which separate them from others but they cannot be said to have control over their own congregations under the Presbyterian form of church government. There is a popular argument, you see, that only churches that are "owned and operated" by Blacks, that are free from white authority or interference, can be considered a part of the Black Church in America. It is assumed, therefore, that Black Presbyterianism, like Black Episcopalianism, is upper middle class, lacking friendliness and warmth, and legally owned and operated by white people rather than Black. Black Presbyterians are, in other words, outside the pale.

Now there are undoubtedly some Black Presbyterians who are quite satisfied about that. They *want* to give the impression that their churches are "better" than, more "high class" than most other churches in the Black community. There is abroad a kind of myth of exclusiveness among some Black Presbyterians. But they are wrong.

Most Black Presbyterian congregations may be somewhat more formal and may lack some of the ardor of a Baptist or Methodist church, but Black Presbyterianism, as a whole, is a constituent part of what we must call the Black Church. With few exceptions, its class status today is no different from most African Methodist or mainline Baptist churches. Historically they cannot be separated from such churches. The First African Presbyterian Church of Philadelphia, as we have seen, was founded before the city's first independent Black Baptist congregation, and nine years before the ecclesiastical compact that created the African Methodist Episcopal Church. Although it had powerful white support, it was, nevertheless, made up of people who had much the same intentions and aspirations as those who followed Richard Allen out of the white Methodist Church. They wanted a church of their own, free from the restrictions imposed by worshiping under the same roof with whites and being deprived, thereby, of the full-standing leadership of their own preachers and lay leaders. John Gloucester was as much a part of Black church leadership in Philadelphia as Allen himself, although he did not have the following enjoyed by the man who was to become bishop of the most powerful Black institution in America. But all of the Philadelphia clergy knew one another in those days. They participated in the same uplift and benevolent causes. They worked together across denominational lines during most of the nineteenth century.

The white presbytery exercised the same formal jurisdiction over its Black as its white congregations. The Presbyterian system required as much, and it must be said that Blacks enjoyed more participation in that system than, for example, the Episcopalians did in theirs. But it was also true that they experienced many instances of discrimination. In the South the situation was worse. When David Laney was ordained by

Hopewell Presbytery he was required to promise that he would restrict his preaching to Blacks only, although he is reputed to have said afterward, "I'll preach to any damn body I please." Even in the North, Black Presbyterians suffered indignities, were overlooked by their white counterparts, and were generally considered marginal to the mainstream of the denomination.

It is not surprising, therefore, that even though they identified with a white denomination, Black clergy and laity were organizing themselves into an ethnic caucus before the end of the nineteenth century. The history of Blacks within the Presbyterian Church will clearly support our contention that their congregations and separate judicatories were always a part of what is recognized as the Black Church in the United States. It is unthinkable that they should be designated in any other way.

But what about the second allegation—that the Black Presbyterian constituency is on a higher socioeconomic level than their brothers and sisters in the Baptist and Methodist churches? That may have once been true, but it is no longer true today. We have no national surveys that can conclusively prove the case one way or another, but local studies and the experience of working in the Black community for many years would seem to dispute the position that Black Presbyterians are an island unto themselves. They are very much a part of the main. Statistics show that the Black Church, taken as a whole, has changed considerably over the past forty or fifty years. Today it is primarily a middle-class institution—despite appearances to the contrary. Black Presbyterian clergy will show a higher level of formal education than their counterparts in other Black churches, but in terms of income, homeownership, social status, the value of church property, and the style of life and individual aspiration, there will not be a great deal of difference between Presbyterians and others. In these indices most Black Christians, particularly in urban areas, look very much like the general American middle class.

Understanding Who We Are Today

The Black Church in America is middle class, and Presbyterians are deceiving themselves if they think that they have an exclusive right to claim that status. This is not to say that there are no more poor people in the Black Church. The underclass is still present—right alongside the middle class, which is usually not true in white churches—but the underclass is no longer dominant. We are no longer preaching on Sunday mornings to a group of poor, oppressed Black people who may not have had a decent meal on Saturday. Whether Baptist, Methodist, Presbyterian, or Congregational, we are ministering to people who, after certain adjustments for the difference between Black and white norms, belong to that great and growing company of taxpayers who enjoy what is called the middle-class American Way of Life. We may not be happy about that, and there are some things we need to do about it, but that is the case today and we need to face it squarely in order to understand who we are and where we are going.

The June/July issue of the magazine *Dollars and Sense* reported in 1981 that more than 20 million Black churchgoers contributed $1.7 billion to their churches. There were five million active members in regular attendance who owned and operated 65,000 separate church properties worth $10.2 billion. When the average Black minister preaches from Luke 4:18 today—"The Spirit of the Lord is upon me, because he has anointed me to preach good news to the poor"—people in the pews look around to see whom he is talking about. When the preacher denounces the unjust, capitalistic system of the United States and calls upon Christians to take a stand against it, he or she may be offending most of the congregation. They are, after all, benefiting from that system and more and more of them have a negative reaction to revolutionary ideas about changing it.

This has been true of African Methodist and the larger

Baptist churches for some time, but today it is also more or less true of The Church of God in Christ, the Seventh-day Adventists, the Pentecostal Assemblies of the World, and the former Nation of Islam (now called the American Muslim Mission). These denominations too, like the more traditional ones, increasingly exhibit the income and even the educational levels, family stability norms, individualism, and optimistic outlook that makes them middle-class institutions in any ordinary sense of the term. As far as social status is concerned, the Presbyterians, the Episcopalians, or the most fashionable Baptist congregations may be a notch or two above them, but in terms of self-image and orientation, what were formerly regarded as backward, fundamentalistic sects are full-fledged churches today. They take their leadership in the community right alongside the older churches and often show a more progressive spirit in the pursuit of justice.

Are There Meaningful Differences Among Blacks?

Although the answer to "Are there meaningful differences among Blacks?" is both yes and no, we should give more weight to the affirmative if we want to get to the bottom of what is wrong with Black Presbyterianism. If we take the Black urban Methodist and Baptist congregations as the norm of the majority of Black churches and ask whether there are noteworthy differences between them and the typical Black Presbyterian congregation, we open up another kind of discussion than the one about class. Black churches of the traditional Black denominations are different from the Presbyterians in three significant areas which we must discuss—historical consciousness, self-image or identity in relation to white people, and ethos. There are, of course, notable exceptions to this, and the reader will have to judge whether or not his or her particular congregation fits the picture that is being drawn.

Even though most Black Baptist and African Methodist churches are middle class, they still have a sense of historical continuity and relationship to a Black past—to the early development of the National Baptist Convention, Inc., or what was called the "Boyd Convention," if they are Baptist. If they are Methodist, they will hark back to some of the great bishops and annual conferences of African Methodism. Because these churches did not inherit their buildings from formerly all-white congregations (as is true of many Presbyterian churches in the North), or subsist for many years on the largess of white mission funds (as is true of many in the South), they have a memory of the past that is "closed" in the sense that it does not include entangling relationships with white people. They have no recollection, generally speaking, of negotiations, visitations, judicatory contacts, educational materials, training sessions, and camps and conferences in which white people played the major and commanding role. These churches have been, for the most part, enclosed in a Black history that may only go back as far as the early years of this century, but they are rooted in and conditioned by the enormous institutionalization of the Black Church during this period. They have a "national Black past." They have a memory of the heroes of that past and a sense of the bonds by which they continue to be bound to them and influenced by them. It is a fact that most Black Presbyterian churches lack this memory, except on a very local level. They have no memory, and therefore no consciousness, of an independent origin and existence inseparable from Afro-American people as a whole and disengaged from the history of white people. We hasten to say that this is more true of Black Presbyterian churches in the North than in the South.

Secondly, the historic Black churches carry an image of themselves that grows not so much out of the conventions of middle-classism in white America as out of an independent past. Their identity may not be as sharp as it should be under the circumstances, but it is usually not confused. When one speaks of a "Black religious tradition" in the Wheat Street Baptist Church in Atlanta or Mother Bethel AME Church in

Philadelphia, the words have a ring of authenticity needing no explanation. Indeed, an explanation may get a raised eyebrow among people who already assume that they are Black and that they belong to the Black community, participating in its characteristics—both positive and negative. Such is not usually the case in Black Presbyterian churches. More often than not, there is a confused identity, a self-image that is, at best, incomplete and, at worst, completely mixed up with what Presbyterianism usually means for white people. When one asks what a congregation looks like when it is both Black and Presbyterian, most Black Presbyterians find it difficult to respond and some might even resent the question.

Thirdly, the ethos or spiritual climate of the historic Black churches is that of what is called the "old-time religon," rather than the enlightened liberalism of a mainline white denomination such as the Presbyterian Church. The ambience of traditional Black churches is, in other words, "down-home" southern, rural, perfectionist, and evangelistic—despite increasing secularizing influences. There is a sort of "Black twist" to all of these aspects of Protestant evangelicalism which makes the ethos feel like something other than mainline white Protestant. One would not, for example, mistake the worship service and congregational life of an AME Zion or Church of God in Christ congregation with those of a white United Methodist or American Baptist church. Whatever is meant by "that old-time religion" in both white and Black churches today—spirited preaching, extemporaneous prayer, sentimental, individualistic hymns, literalism in Biblical interpretation, emotionalism, and an emphasis on the conventional morality of Middle America—is normative for a large number of congregations that belong to traditional or historic Black denominations. But there is a difference between the Black and the white version of "that old-time religion."

In either case, much of the old life-style is gone. There is, we must recognize, an increasing contradiction between what many of these congregations preach and what they practice.

Certain modern adjustments have been made in the "old-time religion" orientation from Monday through Saturday. Nevertheless, the preachers and the laity seem blandly accommodated to the contradiction in a way that Black Presbyterians and Episcopalians are not when they like to think of themselves in this category. As one Church of God in Christ minister said to the writer: "I don't believe in no seminary training as necessary to be a preacher. Seminary can even ruin the whoop of a Black preacher. But I sure would like your help in some of those seminary subjects you fellows teach up there." Not only had he reconciled himself to the contradiction of wanting a seminary education while disparaging it, he was willing to take on the enormous task, in his case, of qualifying for admission. He began in a special program for nonseminary clergy and approached the work with a certain pragmatism and an innocence that was without guile. "Most of these courses," he said,"are like somebody eating fish. You have to eat the meat and spit the bones out."

This attitude is not untypical. Many old-style Black ministers are gradually shifting away from the conservative ethos of the mainline Black tradition and have accepted the necessity of a change without feeling guilty about it. These folks know who they are and where they are going. There is little confusion in their minds about their identity as Black Christians. They are immersed in the culture of the Black community, but they are constantly making adjustments in their way of life to meet the ambiguities of the present without losing the securities of the past. In contast, many Black Presbyterians either lack self-consciousness enough to be naive about what has happened to them psychologically or are painfully aware of the tension between a Black religious past and some vague idea about what it takes to be genuinely Presbyterian. Such people know that there must be some justification for their being Presbyterians, but they are not sure what it is when it permits them, at the same time, to affirm their roots in the Black religious tradition.

We are not prepared at the moment to make value judgments about the differences we have explored. That will come later. We merely want to make the point that there are differences and that some of them are important enough to induce what we would call an identity crisis among Presbyterians that Baptist, Methodist, and Pentecostal people may never experience until they too venture outside the ethos of the community. It is the position of this book that such a crisis is necessary for intelligent and thoughtful Black Presbyterians who want to get themselves together—to sing the Lord's song in a strange land. And when they do, they may have more to contribute to the coming world Church than most congregations of the predominantly Black denominations.

Diagnosis of an Identity Crisis

Our argument is, therefore, that while Black Presbyterians share much of the increasingly middle-class orientation of other Black Christians today, they are cut off from the historic tradition of Black Christianity. Because of that fact, they stand in a more critical situation. In preaching, music, liturgy, polity, patterns of congregational participation, and styles of individual and group behavior, they are not exactly Black and not exactly white. They are somewhere in between. The fact is that most Black Presbyterians are perfectly at home in this situation because they are not sufficiently aware of the deprivation of an identity to be troubled about not having one. Without really being conscious of doing so, they have bought into an unreflective, white middle-class religiosity in which the semblance of commitment too often becomes a substitute for substance. The church and the country club merge into each other. The church becomes a parenthesis between eleven and twelve o'clock on Sundays mornings, the Black cultural and communal experience becomes segmental rather than integrated by a meaningful religious faith, and theological and ideological questions such as "What does it mean in concrete terms to be a human being?" and "What does it mean to be Black and Presbyterian?" have no answer.

Some Presbyterians, in other words, have a problem without knowing it. Much more fortunate are those who have begun to suffer from this problem of a double identity and are beginning to ask how to get rid of the pain and the guilt. We would say that they have entered into the first stages of an identity crisis. Such a crisis is necessary for Black Presbyterians to find themselves and begin to make a contribution to the Black Church and to the whole church of Christ which others, because of the ironies of history, may not be so well equipped to perform. But before going on, let us deal with the key question: What is an identity crisis?

An identity crisis is a critical event in the development of a person or group when a decision is made either to affirm or to deny a historical individuality. By historical individuality we mean that distinctiveness, that uniqueness, which belongs to someone in a particular place, at a particular time, under a particular set of circumstances which all go into making that person who she or he is. Racial and cultural groups, as well as persons, have an identity of their own given by genetic, cultural, and historical factors. When a person or a group asks, "Who am I?" or "Who are we?" a crisis of identity may already have begun in which a decision or judgment is called for before the crisis is resolved and awareness becomes more or less fixed. Usually something internal or external precipitates such a crisis. But in any case, when a person or a group answers the question of identity in terms that entail a *rejection* of an answer that was imposed by another person or group, we may be sure that there is a crisis for both sides! Each must redefine self in relation to other. That is a healthy state of affairs—absolutely necessary for community.

Every parent knows that a child, at some point, becomes a person in his or her own right. When an infant refuses to take his or her bottle, or unceremoniously shoves a plate of strained peas off the table, you suddenly realize that you have an individual human being on your hands! Frustrations, problems—yes, for everyone concerned. But in those days of infancy there was not much of a crisis. It did not have to be taken too seriously. The real identity crisis comes later when you can no longer use a slap on the wrist, the bribe of candy, a lecture, or the keys to the family car to control your child. When a full-grown person stands up to you, eyeball to eyeball, and tells you where to come off—*that* is an identity crisis!

A Special Responsibility

A crisis of identity is obviously not unique to Black Presbyterians. Many Blacks who lived through the 1960s and understood what was going on have experienced such a crisis. Some have slipped back into a previous condition of cultural anonymity and whitenization without even knowing it. Many others have consciously and unconsciously resisted the crisis to fall back into numbed complacency about the meaning and purpose of the Black experience in America. But those of us who are Christians cannot take this matter of culture and ethnic identity lightly. The issue for the Black Church may be put in these terms: "How can Black Christians use the history, culture, and experience of their historic struggle for freedom, something that is distinctively theirs, to enhance the proclamation of the gospel of Jesus Christ and the manifestation of his power to transform not only Black humanity but the whole human race?" That may seem like a tall order for any group of Christians, but we must remember the word of the Lord to Jeremiah when he commanded him to buy a field in an apparently doomed land: "Is anything too hard for me?" (Jer. 32:27). It well may be that those who have experienced both sides of the color line in churches such as the Presbyterian have special resources and responsibilities not possessed by all members of the Black Church today. But the best utilization of those resources and the faithful discharge of those responsibilities will have to wait upon a crisis of identity. We need to discover what Esther discovered—that God does not want us to abandon our people and that we Black Presbyterians may have "come to the kingdom for such a time as this" (Esth. 4:14).

W. E. B. Du Bois wrote about the situation in which many thoughtful people find themselves. In his masterful *The Soul of Black Folk*, he spoke of Black people having "two souls, two thoughts, two unreconciled strivings; two warring ideals in one dark body, whose dogged strength alone keeps it from being torn asunder." Many of us are conscious of this "twoness," particularly if a considerable part of our life, qualitatively if not quantitatively, has involved moving back and forth between the two worlds. This twoness, this double consciousness, this ambivalence is the source of the identity crisis we are experiencing. But the paradox is that although it defines the nature of our weakness, it also—as Du Bois suggests—includes that "dogged strength" which keeps us "from being torn asunder." His striking way of putting it catches the physical as well as the psychological causes and manifestations of this condition. He might have gone one step farther: the twoness itself can be the *source* of strength. That is to say, the strength of Afro-American people may well come from the gift of being able to combine the best part of two cultures in a new life orientation, a new humanity, and overlaying the whole with an indomitable faith in God which is able to transcend the contradictions and delusions of all human existence.

Here we emphasize religious faith because the ordinary ideals of secularism, no matter how enlightened, lack the emotional depth and compelling motivation necessary to grasp the totality of our being and turn us toward the love and forgiveness without which it is not possible to experience integrity and peace. And what is true for the person is also true for collective humanity. The alienation and the hatred that divide and sicken the world cannot be overcome by secular ideologies, but only by faith in a finite being like ourselves, who is also infinite, who "has broken down the dividing wall

. . . reconciling us both to God in one body through the cross, thereby bringing hostility to an end" (Eph. 2:14,16). Thus, the Christian faith provides Afro-American culture with the spiritual cement by which two cultures—one African and the other Euro-American—are reinterpreted and fused into one: a new Black culture that has the power to inspire and direct Blacks toward the goal of *shalom*—the Hebraic idea of the welfare, the peace, the unity of the whole created order.

The problem of the Black Church as the principal carrier of this "gift of Black folk" (Du Bois) is that one part of it has retained Blackness without the sense of a "cultural vocation" which would give Black people greater purpose and direction, while the other part has been tempted to give up Black culture in the interest of its higher calling to a wider, more universal fellowship. The first is the historic Black denominations; the second is the Black constituency of the predominantly white denominations.

In both instances, the power of the Black religious experience to clarify the human condition and inspire people to transcend the imponderables and contradictions of existence is waived, or remains unused, because that experience only expresses its full potential through its twoness—through the synthesis of its two historic components, in the context of religious faith. Take away faith in God's action in history and both aspects of what we call Afro-American culture collapse. Take away an equal emphasis upon Blackness and its cultural vocation to serve not only the liberation of Black people but the liberation and reconciliation of the whole of estranged humankind, and the Black religious experience is falsified and betrayed. Black theology is an attempt to hold all of this together in some more or less logical system of belief and praxis predicated upon the truth of the revelation of God in Jesus Christ. *It is the ordering of the substance of Black religion and Black culture in the United States in such a way as to evaluate them critically, in the light of, and bring them into coherence with, the gospel.* The consequence of such continuous theological work within the Black Church will be the liberation of Black people, and all people, from racism, poverty, and oppression of every kind. But it is also the end of alienation between Black and white—the reconciliation of the two cultures that have had such a profound influence upon the societies of the western hemisphere and, indeed, upon the modern world.

By "the end of alienation" and "reconciliation" we do not mean what some people loosely call racial integration. Far beyond that, we point to what the apostle Paul meant when he wrote:

> From now on, therefore, we regard no one from a human point of view; even though we once regarded Christ from a human point of view, we regard him thus no longer. Therefore, if any one is in Christ, he is a new creation. (II Cor. 5:16–17)

It is a new creation that is in prospect for a world in which the old enmities and alienations are overcome by the sacrificial gift of Jesus Christ—by, as Paul also says, "the blood of his cross" (Col. 1:20). Is it possible, we ask, that in this great and needful work Black Presbyterians, because of the particular twoness they have experienced in the church and the special gifts they bring, have a distinctive role to play? The answer is, we hope, affirmative. That is, indeed, the basic message of this book. We turn now to some of the ways, or strategies, by which this special role and responsibility may be taken up by Black Presbyterians today.

5
Resources of the Black Christian Tradition

Exodus 4:2–5
Acts 8:26–31
Matthew 25:14–30

We began this book with the story of Inez Jones. Let us return to her for a moment. The time has come to analyze her situation more carefully in order to set the stage for talking about resources that were available to her, but that she unfortunately did not have. You will recall her situation. Inez was a member of a white Presbyterian church and of the presbytery's board of trustees for the oversight of its home for the aged. We left her floundering in confusion. An intelligent, conscientious Black laywoman suddenly finds herself encapsulated, unable to affirm a meaningful role for herself within a white Presbyterian world. What happened to Inez is a classic example of a traumatic experience of the identity crisis. The question was not only "What am I doing here?" but "Who, when you get right down to it, am I? What is the meaning of my Blackness in the context of whiteness?"

Three Elements of the Problem

First of all, Inez was possessed of insufficient information, and therefore was misinformed about the Presbyterian Church. It is true that she borrowed some books from the public library, was guided through them by her pastor, and Reverend Homer, the presbytery executive, plied her with reams of material about the mandate for Mulberry Manor. But she was effectively *whitewashed*. Nothing she read had anything to say about Blacks and the Presbyterian Church, except to assert that the church was nonracist and had done many things to encourage Black people to join. This informational emptiness comes as no surprise. With the exception of one or two, none of the scores of books available on the favorite topics—Calvin in Geneva, Knox's struggle with Mary Stuart, the development of the church in colonial America, struggles over the Westminster Confession, revivals and schisms, etc.— include information on who were the *Black* Presbyterians, what did *they* contribute to the church, and how do *they* assess their role in the church today? Her pastor did not know enough to ask about it. It would never have occurred to him that anyone would ask such questions. And that is not to fault him unduly. Pete Manning was a good, liberal Princeton Seminary graduate. He was deeply regretful about the whole thing when the story became known.

Until recently there was nothing a white or a Black pastor could recommend to help the laity understand where Blacks fitted into the Presbyterian scheme of things. There is very little in print on their struggles within the church and the demands they have laid upon the successive General Assemblies, synods, and presbyteries. Inez did the best she could. She was well turned out as a white Presbyterian, ill equipped as a Black one.

Secondly, without that kind of information, or some special counsel and guidance, Inez could not make the decision about herself that she needed to make: whether or not—in her own person—to follow the historic role and function of being Black within the Presbyterian Church. She was not even aware, until it was almost too late, that some kind of decision about that was appropriate. She might have reasoned like so many others: "Well, why make such a big thing about it? Fighting for one's race and joining a church are, or *ought* to be, two different things. Just get in there and be a good Christian—like everybody else."

But it is precisely this question which some literature, or

some good advice, might have clarified. Being a "good Christian" ought to have something to do with following Christ and those faithful men and women who followed him in their day. The Letter to the Hebrews tells us that "we have this large crowd of witnesses around us" (Heb. 12:1, *Good News Bible*) in order that there might be an unbroken communion among all of the Lord's followers. We cannot be good Christians, or for that matter good Presbyterians, unless we take history seriously and know how God acted with and in behalf of those who preceded us. That will have something to do with his gifts and commands to us today. As Black men and women, we have a special history within this denomination that must be appropriated in order that "this large crowd of witnesses" shall not have labored in vain.

On the basis of the meaning of Black presence within the denomination and American Christianity as a whole, Black Presbyterians need to make a choice about whether they intend to carry on and enhance the tradition, or abandon it to the archives. The drifting uncertainty—or, more frequently, indifference—with which some Christians take church membership is unworthy of the Savior and his plan for the salvation of the world. The option is open to each of us. We need to know the truth. And then we need to make up our minds about our personal vocation within this predominantly white church. Will we try to serve Christ and the best interests of Presbyterianism out of the Black religious heritage that has come down to us, or will we simply melt into the woodwork and be just another whitenized, middle-class pew sitter—an "Oreo Presbyterian"? That may sound like hard talk, but discipleship is a serious business. Each of us has the right to have his or her decision respected—whatever it may be in good faith. But decide we must. Inez Jones had no basis for making such a decision before she was deep into a crisis. That is the shame of our casual way of introducing people to the Presbyterian Church—and failing to nurture them afterward.

Thirdly, Inez was isolated. It is difficult enough to be the only Black member of anything—a congregation, a presbytery committee, a board of trustees—but it is so much the worse when one is bereft of outside contacts: the support and good counsel of a citywide or regional chapter of Black Presbyterians United, for example, or some solidarity-conscious group that can help one make choices, set goals, and find bearings. Incidentally, the matter of isolation has no particular implications for whether or not Inez and Tom should have joined a white Presbyterian congregation in the first place. It is just as possible to be isolated in many Black congregations. In the future, increasing numbers of Blacks will become members of predominantly white churches and very likely the reverse will also be true, given the "gentrification" of the core of many metropolitan areas. The question of isolation has to do with the lack of an intentional community of concern and commitment to the Black Christian tradition outside the typical congregation—be it Black or white. Can such a community be found? How significant is one for faithful discipleship in our time?

Black Presbyterians United

In Chapter 3 we looked at the reason for the organization of Black Presbyterians United, and how caucuses have been a part of Presbyterian history almost continuously since the Civil War. The tides of fortune ebb and flow for BPU, but there is, in the early 1980s, a national office and regional structures that attempt to coordinate the activities of local chapters scattered across the nation. If not actually, then potentially, BPU represents a place where someone like Inez Jones could get help—if nothing more than a sympathetic ear and some literature. It is not, and should not be taken as, a shadow church, a substitute Black church within the white church. Nor should it become a rescue mission for all the lonely militants who need to reassure themselves of how Black they are and, at the same time, have a good social time at national and regional gatherings. That too would be a betrayal of all those who fought a good fight and kept the faith to give Blacks a salient and substantive role within the denomination—not just to frighten white people and promote a revolutionary chic.

Black Presbyterians United, at its best, is a society dedicated to the struggle for justice and equality within the denomination. One of its tasks is to make all Presbyterians aware of the resources of the Black Christian tradition and the mission of the Presbyterian Church in the Black community—past, present, and future. Its chapter meetings should be an occasion when a book like this could be discussed and someone like Inez Jones could hear others relate experiences similar to her own. In such a situation she would be challenged to discover ways to coordinate her activities in behalf of First Church and Mulberry Manor with the goals and objectives of other Black Presbyterians in her city.

Is all of this necessary today? Anyone who takes the time to give it more than a casual glance will find that racism still exists within the Presbyterian family, expressed in the attitudes, opinions, and actions of countless individuals whose lives intersect with those of Blacks every day except Sunday. It is institutionalized in decisions about how many and what Blacks should participate in key policy-making structures of the denomination. It is institutionalized in the services that those structures render to church and society. Few Presbyterians think about how covert racism operates, for example, in a home for the aged, a church college or seminary, or the bureaucracies of denominational headquarters. The significance of a national caucus like BPU is that these and other sensitive areas of the church's life are monitored. Intelligent, alert laypeople like Inez Jones are needed in this monitoring system. They help to keep Black congregations aware of what is going on, and they assist the church as a whole to live up to its commitment to racial justice, cultural pluralism, and equal opportunity for all. Unfortunately, Inez did not have the advantage of a Black Presbyterians United chapter and, the goodwill of Manning and First Church notwithstanding, she was isolated in an overwhelmingly white congregation.

What all this boils down to is the fact that Inez Jones was thrown into disarray and neutralized because she had no bearings. She could not claim the white tradition and she was disengaged from the Black. She asked herself, "What am I doing here?" because she was unaware of what needed to be done, what had been the experience of others in the same situation, and—even though she had once been a member of a traditional Black congregation—what were the resources of the Black Christian tradition. Those resources would have given her a *posture* and a *praxis* for meaningful discipleship, and greater confidence in what she and her husband had taken on for themselves when they moved from a Black Baptist to a white Presbyterian congregation.

Five Resources of the Tradition

We have looked at three aspects of Inez Jones's problem. Let us now go directly to the point and examine five resources or elements of the Black Christian tradition with which people like Inez Jones need to be equipped if the gospel is to be proclaimed and demonstrated out of the historic experience that Afro-American people have had with God. If Black Presbyterians have any special gift to bring to the treasury of Christian faith, it is the gift of faith filtered through the American pilgrimage. The whole church of Christ can use these resources of Black faith. Without them—without the witness of men and women who understand and embrace these resources—the American churches, Black and white, will be the poorer. And part of that poverty will consist in the fact that many white Christians will be unable to learn of their own ethnocentrism and be challenged to accept cultural pluralism. Black Presbyterians need to lay claim to and share with others the following resources which are basic to the tradition we have been discussing.

1. Personal and Group Freedom

Freedom from white control is the keystone of the Black religious edifice. It was the reason for the preacher-led slave revolts, the "invisible institution" that met under the brush arbors of southern plantations, the schism of Allen and the African Methodists, and the emptying of the Southern Methodist and Baptist churches after the Civil War. Throughout the history of the Black Church in America the desire for liberty, for the end of white tutelage, paternalism, and domination, has been the driving force of its collective self-consciousness.

The desire for personal and group freedom is rooted and grounded both in the humanity of Blacks and in their understanding of the essential meaning of "If the Son makes you free, you will be free indeed" (John 8:36). It is expressed in the struggle to throw off their bonds, to find a time and space for themselves within which they could exercise the freedom of body and soul, and in the way they mobilized and organized themselves for many generations, mainly through the church, to press for their own liberation and that of brothers and sisters in Africa and the Caribbean. Without an emphasis on freedom and liberation the Black Christian tradition is without its anchor in Jesus Christ, for he is the Liberator *par excellence*, and it was because of the freedom Blacks found in him that their churches were called into existence.

2. The Image of Africa as the Land of Origin

Historically, the Black Church has thought of itself as an *African* rather than a "Negro" Church. It is significant that no denomination used the latter term in its name, but many used the former. We sometimes exaggerate the importance of this connection with Africa today. But it is still true that authentic Black religion carries a mystique about Africa as a place of origin. This mystique includes a recognition of God's dealings with Africa (particularly with Egypt, Ethiopia, and Nubia) in the Old and New Testament periods, and the expectation that Africa will someday be vindicated for her humiliation and despoliation, and attain the greatness of her ancient past. Many of the sermons and essays of Black preachers in the nineteenth century repeated these themes over and over. Benevolent societies and fraternal orders emphasized and ritualized this image of Africa—that place in the world where the culture and spirit of the Black race could be freely expressed and esteemed. Black colleges and universities taught African history when it was unknown in other institutions. They took pains also to bring African young men and women to the United States to receive higher education and return home to help their people.

The first missionary outreach of the Black Church was to the African continent. The redemption of Africa was the rallying cry of Black Christians throughout the nineteenth century, and many leaders, like Bishop Henry McNeal Turner of the AME Church, believed that it was God's will for Afro-Americans to return to the land of their ancestors.

Despite the work of religious Black nationalists and others in the community, Africa has not occupied the place in Black religion and culture in the twentieth century that it enjoyed in the nineteenth. But it is still a part of the tradition, as anyone will learn who investigates where the troops come from for Pan-Africanist causes, such as the liberation of Southern Africa. Behind the movement for Black consciousness and solidarity in the churches is the assumption that God did not leave our non-Christian ancestors without a witness. Within the indigenous religions of Africa there remain values which Black Christians and other religionists of the Diaspora need to reclaim. The consciousness of Africa and things African skyrocketed in the 1960s through the work of the National Conference of Black Churchmen and other Christian groups. It may be somewhat less prominent in the churches today. But it is still a part of the tradition.

3. The Will of God for Social Justice

A third powerful resource of the Black Christian tradition is the undisputed assumption of most churches in which Afro-Americans predominate that it is the will of God and the business of the church to be engaged in the struggle for justice and human rights as a normal part of what it means to be a Christian. The commitment goes back to the first organized churches that supported abolitionism and helped to create the Underground Railroad. There was an early expectation that Black ministers had to be "race men." They were expected to use the political and economic power of the churches to defend the rights of the widow and the orphan, "to loose the bonds of wickedness, to undo the thongs of the yoke, to let the oppressed go free, and to break every yoke" (Isa. 58:6).

The idea that religion and politics do not mix, which one often finds in white congregations, is contrary to the tradition of Black Christianity. Black preachers of the nineteenth century knew their Old Testament. What impressed them was how "Daniel's God" acted in the affairs of his people. The Negro spirituals express the exploits of the Lord of hosts and the intervention of "King Jesus" in behalf of those who are despised and abused in this world. As much as many contemporary Black churches, moving into the middle class, may attempt to underplay this emphasis, it continues to rise up in times of resurgent racism, poverty, and unemployment to force them to return to the political arena or suffer the ridicule and contempt of the masses.

The power of clergymen like Adam Clayton Powell, Jr., Martin Luther King, Jr., and Jesse Jackson gives testimony to the historic commitment of the Black Church to the struggle for social justice. That commitment may flag as some Black Christians join the ranks of the oppressors and turn up in television programs sponsored by the reactionary evangelists of the Moral Majority. But the radical tradition runs deep in the ghetto, and it continues to be motivated and inspired by the religion of the masses.

4. Creative Style and Artistry

Much has been written about this resource, but there has been comparatively little investigation of style and artistry as elements of the Black religious tradition. It is difficult to describe and analyze in a few words. Anyone, however, who has observed the style of preaching, the prayers and testimonies, music, and general behavioral characteristics of the typical Black congregation on a Sunday morning has probably been struck with its spectacular quality.

The Black worship service is a theater of the divine. There is great performatory power in what on the surface may appear to be careless informality, but in fact is an intentionally crafted and stylized pattern of pastoral leadership and congregational participation. People find worship exciting and entertaining as well as edifying and enlightening. In the aesthetic of the Black Christian tradition the "beauty of holiness" is not restricted to the consecrated nature of the ritual, or contemplation of the perfections of God enthroned in majesty. It involves our human ability and skill in the execution of worship so that what takes place makes God real, not only invokes him, but does it with finesse and artistry. The event of worship becomes something joyously satisfying to behold and participate in. Black folks come out of church talking about how much they "enjoyed" the service. They emerge with a sense of having participated in something special, in the drama of salvation. The preacher, the robed, swinging choirs, the colorful congregation become the dramatis personae who have a flair about how they "call and respond" to each other, smoothly coordinating roles, and entering into a symbolic enactment of "the story"—the message that has held the community together through thick and thin, and gives it identity and "a concert of sympathies" (Ralph Ellison).

This creative style and artistry is a cultural artifact. It is part of what Afro-American ethnicity is all about, and it is rooted in the African inheritance. In a broader cultural context it is found in the oral tradition, music, dress, cuisine, and general savoir-faire of many people who are immersed in the Black community. It is expressed specifically in the Black religious experience in terms of innovativeness in Biblical interpretation and preaching, improvisation in church music, spontaneity in worship (within prescribed limits), and—in the most sophisticated urban churches—a subtle balance between emotional and intellectual content. It is something that Black Presbyterian churches often lack because of having chosen to emulate the middle-class white religious community. But one detects a change since the 1960s. More Black Presbyterian congregations are rediscovering the distinctive aesthetic and artistry of this tradition.

5. The Unity of Secular and Sacred

In this fifth and final resource of the tradition, we are dealing with the substructure, the groundwork upon which all the others rest. Most scholars are in agreement that the erasure of the line between the secular and the sacred, the profane and the holy, everyday life and fervid religion, is a basic characteristic of African religions. Many would go farther to say that it is probably the most significant part of those religions brought to the American continent by the African slaves. The world view based upon the unity of the secular and the sacred is a characteristic of all African and Afro-American societies which have not been almost totally acculturated to the perspective of those who belong to societies more conditioned by the Enlightenment and the scientific revolution. The habit of dividing reality up into two parts, and consigning the smaller to things "religious," seems endemic to Euro-American civilization. The sharp dichotomy between religion and the rest of life was not known in Africa, and though it was greatly weakened in North America before 1750, the unified or holistic perspective continued for a long time to embody the folk tradition.

This does not mean that Black folk did not recognize a difference between "praying and plowing," or that for them everything existed in a divinized world that rejected the intrusion of reason and scientific method. That would be an extreme primitivism. All religions may have passed through such a stage in their evolution. The question at issue here is whether or not "the baby was thrown out with the bath water" as religious beliefs developed and matured under modernity. Black Christianity, with its African background, may have been more successful than its white counterpart in assimilating the world view of the Bible with the modern scientific view. When we spoke earlier about a "pragmatic spirituality" as characteristic of a large sector of the Black Church, we were trying to describe this particular brand of religious worldliness which has no difficulty using the church as much for winning strikes and elections as winning souls. There may be a better way of putting it, but pragmatic spirituality suggests a different orientation than the one based upon the assumed polarity of the holy and worldly aspects of life.

Black religion and folklore have shown, nevertheless, a persistent tolerance for the mysterious and the occult. Many Black Christians still believe that the spiritual is pervasive in our world, and behind the one we can see and handle there exists an invisible world that is no less real and efficacious in our daily life. It is not difficult to see that such a view coheres well with that of Scripture. The miraculous power of Jesus and his disciples is taken for granted, for the inauguration of his Lordship means that God had changed things, "delivered us from . . . darkness and transferred us to the kingdom of his beloved Son" (Col. 1:13). Black people for whom the church is important believe that they already live in a "new creation" where God is not governed by the laws of science. He is free to supersede such laws in the interest of a cosmic "redemption, the forgiveness of sins" as well as establish them for our ordinary daily life.

Religion, from this perspective, has to do with all of life, and all of life has to do with religion. The same beat that stirs our souls when the "good times roll" on Saturday night stirs them in another context on Sunday morning. Aretha Franklin learned how to sing the blues by singing gospel. Martin Luther King, Jr., could march thousands to the picket line with the same music and much of the same spirit with which he marched them down the aisle of Black churches in Selma, Alabama, or Washington, D.C. To say that Afro-American people are "a religious people" (*Message to the Churches from Oakland*, National Conference of Black Churchmen, Nov. 14, 1969) is not to say that we are still living in a precognitive world, relying on magic and charms while others use reason and technology. It simply means that we do not believe that God is dead, and as believers it is incumbent upon us to find appropriate ways to serve a living God. We have learned, through suffering and struggle, to praise him while passing the ammunition. We are, at one and the same time, a religious people who are not afraid to look hard reality in the face, and a secular people who have believed the gospel.

Preserving the Values of Black Faith

These are the major resources of the tradition that has always been available to Black Christians who would reach out into the history and culture of their people to claim it. Not enough has been written about the continuing virtue of this kind of religion in the Black community. It is, nevertheless, firmly rooted in many of our churches and institutions. Whether it will continue to enrich the life of the masses, not to mention that of the new middle class, will depend in large measure upon how much the organized Black Church is prepared to invest in retaining it as the thrust of its cultural vocation. Thousands of Black laymen and laywomen need reorientation to this understanding of the tradition if it is to be preserved and enhanced rather than permitted to disappear into oblivion. That is a task for Christian education at every level—from the Sunday school to the theological seminary.

It is not a matter of canonizing these resources of Black

religion and refusing to admit that there is any other way for Black people to apprehend the truth about nature, human-kind, and God. We believe in a progressive revelation—the unfolding of truth as persons and groups encounter one another in dialogue around issues that require real decisions and commitments. But Black Christians do not, as was supposed by some, come to such dialogues empty-handed. A long experience of becoming a people, of trial and testing, struggle and sacrifice on the way to "the Promise Land," has deposited a wealth of secular wisdom and religious insight in the stream of Black culture. We dare not ignore this, or treat it lightly. American culture and religion have become so indi-vidualistic that everyone is doing his or her "own thing," and folkways and group traditions are considered by many to be stultifying and anachronistic. Our society can use a greater emphasis upon some of the values and customs of the folk community. It is one of the gifts of Black folk that they appreciate the nature and importance of peoplehood. They need, therefore, to be encouraged not simply to hold on to these values from the past, but build upon them for the present and the future. Both unconsciously and by deliberate effort, American culture and society as a whole is likely to benefit from a revitalization of religion and culture in the Black community.

Inez Jones *did* have a reason for being on the board of Mulberry Manor and something significant to do there . It did not require that she explode into a paroxysm of "Black talk" to prove how radical she was or how uncoopted by her new white friends. Nor did it require that she resign and return to the Black Baptist congregation where she was brought up. God could use this talented, searching person to clarify the mean-ing of the Black Christian tradition and contribute to its contemporary enrichment. The presbytery needed what that tradition has to offer, if only to challenge and rejuvenate the few struggling Black congregations within its bounds. No, Inez Jones could have been a definite asset to many people, Black and white, in that situation. And it would not have called for some of the raw confrontational tactics that were needed in the 1960s. Today we have a greater knowledge of what we have and a greater ability to commend it to others. The desperateness of the world in which we live may make for an unusual openness in the white community—particularly in the inner city which is becoming increasingly interracial in some of the most strategic areas of the nation.

Unfortunately, our story does not have an altogether happy ending. Inez did, as a matter of fact, drift away from First Church. She subsequently resigned from the board of Mulberry Manor and no longer worships anywhere with the old regularity and enthusiasm. And she has not found a chapter of Black Presbyterians United to which she feels that she can relate, although there is one in her city. In some ways this young woman found herself by being honest about how she felt about being "on display" in this particular situation. But she has not yet found a Christian community that can explain and sustain the ambiguities she still feels about being Black in a predominantly white church. Perhaps this book will help her. To all of the Inezes out there: You know who you are. You can go home again, even in a predominantly white church. You should, at least, replenish your provisions by stopping by home before continuing your faith journey.

6
Toward a New Style
of Black Presbyterianism

Hebrews 11:32–40
I Thessalonians 4:9–12
Joshua 24:1–28

Dr. James H. Costen, Moderator of the 194th General Assembly and dean of Johnson C. Smith Theological Seminary in Atlanta—our one surviving predominantly Black Presbyterian theological school—has made a study of the health and welfare of Black Presbyterianism in the United States. His diagnosis is good. Costen's prediction for the future is surprisingly optimistic. His statistics bear out our earlier contention about the middle-class status of the Black constituency. Moreover, much of what Costen writes suggests that in terms of per capita giving, levels of schooling, membership growth by congregations, and the relative numbers of persons in top leadership positions at regional and national church levels, Black Presbyterians are out in front of the denomination. He wrote in 1976: "Perhaps chauvinistically, I am ready to say with great passion that Black Presbyterians are giving to the United Presbyterian Church its finest hour in almost one hundred years. The church needs to know this."

For those who are weary of the self-deprecation and inferiority complexes among us, this is reason enough for celebration. Black Presbyterians can hold their heads high. In 1976, in the United Presbyterian Church 72,698 gave $13,013,086 to the denomination. Indeed, 1,099 fewer Black Presbyterians gave $54,249 more in 1974 than in 1973 and, in all probability, that trend continues into the 1980s. The average per capita giving in 1974 was $63 more than the average Protestant, and $12 more than the average white Presbyterian church member gave.

These figures do not tell us all we need to know about our socioeconomic situation relative to other Black Christians, or to our white counterparts in the Presbyterian Church. But they do suggest that while Black Presbyterians may not yet be living in paradise, they are in a state of well-being compared to many other groups in the United States—for example, the poor Blacks of the rural South, the Puerto Ricans, Native Americans, Haitians, and some of the more recent arrivals from Southeast Asia. A little better than a casual observation of many of our congregations would note that their members have as many or more college degrees than most congregations, are in as good health, as well-dressed and well-driven as most white Presbyterians anywhere in the nation. Their wealth may not be old and deep, like that of some of the "avenue churches" in New York City and Washington, or some of the more fashionable congregations in Texas and California, but it is sufficient to give one a picture of comfort and complacency, despite the shameful way the salaries of the clergy and the material needs of the properties may be neglected year after year. Indeed, Black Presbyterians continue to be embarrassed by stories of congregations still operating out of a welfare mentality, still looking to presbytery to bail them out of some financial difficulty.

Can Any Good Thing Come Out of Black Presbyterianism?

While some of us are cheered by Costen's studies, others are dismayed. If we are no longer in the ranks of the poor, can we be expected to participate in the great struggle of the Black masses for the completion of their liberation? Do we have anything distinctive to offer anyone, other than the same indifference toward the plight of the oppressed, the same obsession with materialism, and the same conservative attitude about the American economy and foreign policy that one finds among the majority of white Presbyterians?

The question deserves serious consideration. If good jobs, homes that are paid for, children in college, and vacations in the Caribbean disqualify Black Christians for the kind of discipleship we have been discussing in this book, we have wasted our time. Much of what has been said about the resources of the Black Christian tradition must be judged irrelevant as far as Blacks of this particular Church are concerned. Black liberation theologians would take Costen's analysis ruefully. We are, they would say, just the kind of people who were vulnerable to the Nixon Administration's appeal for Blacks to enter into collaboration with the owners of the wealth of corporate America; to pick up the profit margins that trickle down, or fall as savory crumbs from the masters' table. The liberators of the Black masses and the people of the Third World, Black theologians would contend, must be made of sterner stuff. It will not be the elite and affluent of the Black community, but those who are hurting the most—the urban proletariat and the landless farm workers—who will lead the revolution. Since Black Presbyterians rarely fall into the category of the truly needy—the welfare mothers, the agricultural migrants, petty criminals, and thousands of young Black men and women now languishing in prisons—we must be considered a part of the American system of greed and exploitation, part of the machinery of imperialism that grinds the faces of the poor at home, and in Africa, Asia, and Latin America.

Whatever one may think of the cogency of this position, there seem to be only two clear alternatives for us: either to forget the idea of Black Presbyterians being a part of any revitalization of culture and religion that brings the status quo under radical critique, or (and this seems equally doomed to failure) to ask Black Presbyterians to divest themselves of the accouterments of middle-class life and return to the ghetto on the level of brothers and sisters struggling for survival. Actually, there are other possibilities, but these two are the most often heard. The first is crushingly pessimistic; the second, fatuously optimistic and visionary.

The final question that we need to address, and perhaps the most important question in this book, is this: Is there anything in between that would give us some hope that those who are no longer on the bottom can share in Christ's ministry to the poor and oppressed without giving up everything for which they and their ancestors faithfully labored in the heat of the day?

The New Testament Witness

There is no easy answer to this question. The New Testament teaches that wealth is a snare to any pilgrim on the way to the Kingdom of God. Nothing is more difficult than for the rich to enter that Kingdom. Yet no one is rejected solely on that account. There were evidently people of property and prestige among the followers of Jesus and the apostles. Not many, but enough to assure us that they were not categorically excluded. Paul hints several times that he depended upon the generosity of such members of the churches with which he had contact. There must have been a way to own wealth and property in the early church and still remain obedient to the gospel and faithful to the community.

Of course, we must not exaggerate the position of Black Presbyterians today. There is a big difference between being comfortable and being really wealthy. Very few Black Presbyterians are wealthy by North American standards. And we neither think nor live like wealthy people. Like most of the Black middle class, we exist on the brink of financial disaster most of the time, and we have a sharp memory of what it is like to be poor. But the fact remains that the gap between our disposable income and material possessions and those of most of the people in the world is enormous, and getting wider every year. We have to face the fact that we are still a highly privileged group, despite the well-taken and oft-quoted disparities between Black and white in the United States.

In the church of Jesus Christ where "not many . . . were wise according to worldly standards, not many were powerful, not many were of noble birth" (I Cor. 1:26), in a church where the poor heard Jesus gladly because he not only healed them, but reminded them that "yours is the kingdom of God" (Luke 6:20), those who live as well as we do will have an explanation to make when we appear before the judgment with brothers and sisters who have never known what it feels like not to be hungry. Our churches are often found in the midst of people who are ill-fed, ill-clothed, and ill-housed, but it is a rare congregation that is involved in helping such people on a continuing basis. We may not be rich, but we are not poor, and we need to worry more than we do about how it is possible to please God if we continue to indulge ourselves with the things of this world while others suffer daily misery and privation.

Although there are no easy answers to our dilemma, there are several possibilities we need to consider whenever we discuss the meaning of discipleship. Jesus called upon the young man to "go, sell what you possess and give to the poor . . . and come, follow me" (Matt. 19:21), but there is no indication that he made that a general rule. His instructions were tailored for the person and the occasion. He did not press the same requirement upon Levi (Luke 5:27–32), or Zacchaeus (Luke 19:1–10), yet both were obviously quite well off. The same must be said of "the other Mary," the mother of John Mark, whose spacious house was at the disposal of the disciples (Acts 12:12).

One possibility worth considering is John Wesley's advice to his congregation in a sermon on "The Use of Money": "Gain all you can, save all you can, give all you can." Another is to live as if having or not having wealth is no issue, knowing, with Paul, "how to be abased, and . . . how to abound" (Phil. 4:11–13), and how to use whatever we may have for the glory of God. An example would be empowering the poor and dispossessed to throw off their bonds and take responsibility for their own lives in a world of justice and sufficiency for all.

In Search of a New Style of Life

Whatever decision Black Presbyterians may make, with the help of God's Word, prayer, and dialogue, it is likely to be an improvement over the pointless, indifferent way we now deal with the question of privilege and responsibility in the Black community. If we are serious about what it means to be Black middle class and Presbyterian, we will constantly search for a new style of middle-class life in the midst of the poverty of the world around us, a new model of responsibility and loving service to the world for which Christ died.

By "style" we refer to that distinctive mode of living, of personal deportment and collective action, that characteristic form and appearance, whereby a people express who they are and what they value most in this world. Artistic and professional people often have a style about themselves: for example, a jazz musician, or a Metropolitan prima donna "walks, talks, and dresses the part." A popular candidate for political office is said to have "a charismatic style." A physician is said to have "a good bedside manner." Father Divine's followers and the former Black Muslims had distinctive but different styles. So do some Jesus People, adherents of Hare Krishna, members of the Society of Friends, and Mormons.

Style often has to do with communication. People who have a distinctive style of life are usually getting across a message of some sort to themselves and others. If it is done too self-consciously, it can be a mild irritant, like a television game show host who is just too clever and cute. If it is done too unselfconsciously, it can be ambiguous and unpredictable, like young girls in bikinis. Good style is skillfully executed, deliberately projected on the screen of the external world.

That is why we notice it. But it must somehow strike a balance between being studied and "letting it all hang out," as if one could not care less about what people think.

What can be said about the style of most Presbyterians and Episcopalians? Some would say that their style is to have no style. To be as inconspicuous as possible about religious affiliation and commitment, lest they give the impression that they are fanatical about it; to melt quietly into the great mass of middle-class, decent, law-abiding Americans who never behave themselves ostentatiously or raise their voices in public. There is nothing wrong with such a style of life, except its boredom. Its communication potential is minimal and no one learns very much about what such persons are really like.

What we are suggesting is that Christians should have more of a style of life than this, and, since we are discussing a specific group of Christians, that Black Presbyterians need something distinctive and impressive about "the way they walk," to use a good Biblical phrase. They need something that makes them stand out from the run-of-the-mill middle-class American, that expresses what they value and disvalue in life, that communicates to each other and to outsiders how they view the world in the light of what we have been talking about in this book—the gospel filtered through the Black Christian experience. This may sound crafty and too artificial—the substitution of one brand of phoniness for another, but the fact is that in the world of the closing years of the twentieth century nothing less than an exhibition, a decisive display of difference, as opposed to sameness, will grasp public attention and cause people to examine their lives in the light of an arresting alternative to "the American Way of Life." The presentation of oneself and one's group must, of course, be honest. The world will no longer pay attention to what we *say* about ourselves. It is looking for a demonstration of truth—a pantomime of salvation, not a verbal description of it. If Black Presbyterians have anything to say to one another and to the world that will be heard, in spite of the electronic Babel of the false prophets, we will have to live it out with a flair and a style that is not merely affectation, but an honest and joyous habitude that communicates who we are, individually and collectively, and why we think our way of life is the best way to live in this world.

What is wrong with hearing someone say, "From the way they live I would guess they are Presbyterians," or "Only a Presbyterian would take the position she took at that meeting," or "If there were more Presbyterians in this community, we could get some things done"? The point is that it should make a difference when one is a member of a Black Presbyterian congregation, or when there is such a congregation in the neighborhood. People should notice the difference. It should reflect ethos, the moral and aesthetic evaluation of a group of people who are in solidarity with one another about certain understandings and disciplines of life. Such people commend to others their beliefs and way of life by how they carry themselves, by the way they worship, study, and commune with one another and with strangers. They are known by the things that interest them and the things they refuse to be involved in, by the causes they support and those they refuse to support, by the sacrifices they make and the spirit with which they make them. Such people are known by the way they raise their children, use their leisure time, subordinate their individualism in behalf of collective ideals and goals. The world cannot help noticing what kind of employees they make, their different pattern of consumption, their economic self-reliance, their political participation and responsible use of power. In short, they *are* a different brand of humanity, and they are neither ashamed of it nor interested in keeping it a secret.

These indices constitute principles by which one's life is governed as an individual and as a member of a group. Some of them we have filled with content, others we have been vague about, or simply left open. It is important for Black Presbyterians to talk about such things against the background of what we have inherited from the past and what we hope for the future of the Presbyterian Church. Only when we will have developed some consensus about them will a voluntary, internalized style of life begin to emerge that will be truly Black and Presbyterian. In the interest of that devoutly to be wished discussion, we have some specific suggestions about life-style in three areas: leadership, congregational life, and outreach into the wider community.

Leadership

The possibility of Black Presbyterians moving toward a new life-style in the 1980s and 1990s depends, in the first place, upon whether or not our teaching and ruling elders will take the initiative, introducing a new life-style to the congregations and leading the way. Members need a demonstration of what we are talking about. The willingness of trusted leaders and their families to change their own way of life in order to create a new ethos for the congregation will go a long way toward convincing skeptical members that we are serious. There is no substitute for a direct promotion of a change in attitude and behavior in which the minister and the key leaders become primary examples of what is being asked from the people. Unless those who have the trust and respect of the congregation take upon themselves the risks and insecurities of changing old habits, nothing will happen. Books may be read, literature distributed, cassettes listened to, discussion groups formed, but little or nothing will come of all the talk about changing life-style. People will go on in the same old ruts with only minor and tentative changes, if any. And for the most part, the adjustments will be indiscernible to the outside world.

What is being called for here is something much more serious and permanent. Since patterns of consumption and the values that determine them—in other words, economic ethics—are so basic to one's way of life, the leaders must begin on that level, the level of economic decision-making. A commitment must be made on the part of a few families

(families in the broad sense) who are opinion makers in the congregation and willing to enter into some cooperative arrangements for the use of family income. Many Black churches today tithe, and that is certainly a good place to begin. But the leadership must go beyond tithing. The joint purchase of basic food commodities, household cleaning and hardware supplies, appliances, gasoline, and various other items—from golf balls to retirement annuities—will begin to alter the economic patterns of the participants and build up reserves of income that can be used for various enterprises of the congregation. Among them will be those projects which engender the spirit of cooperation, self-determination, and solidarity. Here and there across the nation Black congregations have sponsored money-making enterprises, nonprofit economic development, low-income housing, retirement homes, family camps and rural recreation properties, alternative schools, tutoring programs, day care, and job training programs. A discussion of specific examples would take us afield, but the models exist. It should not be difficult to find them.

What is essential in all such ventures is doubly necessary in this instance when people are being asked to surrender some jealously guarded individual prerogatives in the interest of the group—enthusiasm, clarity of goals and means, honesty and good management, and a sincere religious commitment. People must be impressed with the absolute necessity of forging a new form of discipleship if they and their children are to survive the individualistic, greed-motivated economics of the world in which they live. They must be helped to see that the faith which nurtured and the culture which enriched their ancestors will simply evaporate into the aridity of a crassly materialistic middle-classism unless something drastic is done now. Someone must decide to give up the life-style of getting and spending in a never-ending, self-indulgent pursuit of happiness, opting instead for solidarity in the praxis of liberation.

If pastors, members of session, trustees, and other key leaders will begin the discussion among themselves and take the initiative on a small, manageable scale, many in the congregation will follow. *We need leadership!* And if our churches can show that being Black and middle class does not necessarily mean being like some Black families are depicted on prime-time television shows, or like some happy, hygienic, hedonistic family in the glossy magazines on the counter at the supermarkets, then other churches in the community will do what they did for many years in the South—make the Presbyterian Church a model for their own elevation and development in Christian education and discipleship. One hundred thousand Black Presbyterians in three major denominations do not sound like enough in a Black churchgoing population of about twenty million. But given the state of the Black Church today, relative to the issues we have been discussing, it is a majority! All that is required are people who are willing to provide the role models—to step outside the tight little wall of self and family to enter into cooperative economic and social covenants with others in order to change our way of life, once and for all. It is not true that it is impossible to be middle class and be involved in the revolutionary activity of the Kingdom. Martin Luther King, Jr., was of the *crème de la crème* of Black middle-class society and he enjoyed comfort and prestige, but he gave his life in a struggle for garbage workers in Memphis. Only we can decide what is worth living and dying for. Only we can decide to get out of the rat race and enter that other race "toward the goal for the prize of the upward call of God in Christ Jesus" (Phil. 3:14).

Congregational Life

The focus should begin on worship, Christian education, and evangelism. Of course, what we are calling the new lifestyle of Black Presbyterianism is comprehensive. It has to do with the total expression of what it means to be a baptized person. It is a *curriculum* for Christian living out of the Black cultural and religious tradition. The congregation may be thought of as the larger or outer circle of which the session, in the Presbyterian system, is the inner circle or core. We have just talked about the inner circle, and what we said applies equally to the rest of the congregation. Our point has been that the pastor and the official boards need to introduce the changes and lead others to accept the kinds of convenantal disciplines that they, the leaders, have begun. The outer circle becomes, then, a staging area or pool from which persons are being constantly recruited. But only when they are ready, and not before. A sufficient evidence of readiness would be some indication of having grasped the principles of the new life-style, having reached a recognized level of religious maturity, and having given a voluntary notification of the desire to make a commitment. But this does not mean that we have to wait until at least fifty percent of the people are on board. The whole congregation is already involved in the changes. The areas of congregational worship, Christian education, and evangelism are being drawn into the new ethos emanating from the pastor and the lay cadre. These vital areas should already show the impact of the new ideas being constantly discussed and promoted in the church. What are we driving at in these areas of congregational life?

Worship. Many Presbyterian congregations have already examined their worship services and found them lacking the spirit and excitement of the older tradition. It is no longer unusual to find a mixed style of worship in Black Presbyterian churches. Gospel music alternates with the anthems of the senior choir. There is greater emphasis on bodily movement and congregational participation. In some of our churches "Amens" and "Thank you, Jesus" punctuate the sermon, and there are altar calls and invitations to discipleship. It is not enough, however, simply to copy traditional forms in the same way that we copied the forms of white Presbyterian worship. The pastor and the worship committee should help the congregation become selective about new and creative forms that draw upon Black culture. People need to discuss what we mean by Black liturgy. There should also be some concern about broadening our experience to include liturgical elements from African Christianity and other Third World churches.

Innovations, such as the display of a Black Christ or images of a Black Madonna and Child, remind the congregation of the universality of Christian symbols by particularizing them. New-style Black Presbyterian worship should mean a joyous return to the Afro-American spiritual as an internationally recognized art form sadly neglected by the Black Church today. Some clergy have recently discovered that there is a body of Black "sacred writings," such as certain passages from David Walker, Martin Delany, or Frederick Douglass, the poetry of Countee Cullen and Alice Walker, the words of "Lift Ev'ry Voice and Sing," excerpts from the sermons and speeches of Malcolm X, Martin Luther King, Jr., and Howard Thurman. These are the rich deposits of almost four hundred years of Afro-American religion and culture. Our young people need to know of them. There is no reason why they should not be interpolated into the liturgies of the Black Church.

Imagination and creativity can utilize Black music, the dance, banners, outdoor processionals, dramatic skits in the sanctuary, and liturgical elements from other traditions, to enrich our worship services. Here is one of the best opportunities we have to excite the interest and participation of younger members by helping them to think through the meaning of Black worship, its possibilities for broader and more universal application, and enlisting them as worship leaders and liturgists. This is not to say that there should not be some time for quiet, traditional Presbyterian worship with which the older members of the congregation identify. But there is room for variety and experimentation. We need more of it today.

Christian Education. An entire book could be written on the educational implications of the new life-style. We shall not attempt here to explore all the possibilities. Needless to say, our primary target is the children and young people. What is called for is the kind of comprehensive curriculum which integrates the church school, youth groups, family nights, camps and conferences, and church-sponsored supplements to the public schools, around the central issues of this book: What is the Black Christian tradition? What does it mean to be a Black person and belong to the Presbyterian Church? What is meant by a "new life-style" for those who value Black history and culture and want to use them in worshiping and serving Christ? Several denominations have begun, for the first time, to produce educational resources that open up the relationship between ethnicity and theology, between the culture of the Afro-American community and the gospel. The United Presbyterian Church has the Faith Journey Series, which can be used to introduce children and youth to the Black Christian experience in the context of the contemporary Church. Here again we must depend upon leadership at the local level to motivate people to utilize such material. Those who are leaders must show enthusiasm for these materials and demonstrate their salutary influence upon their own understanding of the faith and their own personal behavior.

Many churches have made excellent use of the weekend family camp or the all-day Saturday church conference. Brief, interesting lectures, followed by small-group discussion, feedback sessions, films, and skits—interspersed with spirited singing and physical exertion—can accomplish more over a six- or eight-hour period than a month of hurried lessons on Sundays. The emphasis should be upon the youth. Adult education should certainly not be neglected, and, in some situations, it may be necessary to begin with parents before reaching that level of trust and understanding which will grant access to their children and young people. The ideal situation is when all grades, oriented to the same core curriculum, proceed simultaneously, interfacing and reinforcing one an-

other in a coordinated, churchwide program of Christian
education. Indeed, a primary aspect of new-style Black Presbyterianism will be the attention it gives to continuous, absorb-
ing educational experiences for the entire congregation.

This is to say that an important, even essential, part of the
new life-style is to be a literate congregation—a "reading
church." By a "reading church" we mean one that is made up
of individuals and families who set great store by their interest
in and mastery of Black history, literature, and theology, as
well as the Bible—a church that has an active lending library,
a book review club, and various kinds of study and discussion
groups that pride themselves on their ability to read and
discuss topics that run the gamut from the current work in
Black feminist theology to the latest Toni Morrison novel. A
reading church is already a church on the way to a new-style
discipleship in the Black perspective. There is much illiteracy
and widespread ignorance of the major texts of Black life and
culture—Du Bois's *The Souls of Black Folk*, James Cone's
Black Theology and Black Power, James Boggs's *Racism and
the Class Struggle*, Thurman's *With Head and Heart*.
Churches that do not know this literature are woefully
uninformed and miseducated. One could safely wager that
their members are getting their cues about ethics and life-style
from the six o'clock television news program and *Ebony*. Both
may be useful for taking the pulse of the times, but they
cannot compete with a systematic, churchwide program that
emphasizes the reading of quality literature.

Evangelism. Black churches have traditionally stressed
evangelism—the sermon calling for a decision, the sawdust
trail, the mourners' bench. But evangelism in new-style
discipleship should have a broader meaning. It should refer to
introducing men, women, and children to Jesus Christ not
only through Scripture and prayer but also by showing them
the revelatory meaning of the Black experience—a meaning
that breaks through our literature, art, music, and political
activity to mark milestones in the journey toward liberation.

God has not only been seeking us as individuals who need "saving," he has pursued the Black nation as a whole in order to make of us a people of his election, a people entrusted with his purposes for all the families of the earth. What that special vocation is all about, its claims upon each of us and how they should be answered in the fellowship of brothers and sisters responding to the same call, is what we mean by new-style evangelism.

This is not to depreciate traditional ways of pleading, admonishing, challenging—opening the "doors of the church," and inviting all present to accept Jesus as their personal Savior. The invitation in the traditional Black liturgy, with its sense of urgency, its direct emotional appeal, and its skillful use of music, is a moving experience and needed in formalistic Black Presbyterian churches. But there is no reason why other methods of introducing persons to Christ cannot be used as well—from the open-air street meetings that Black Presbyterians in Philadelphia sponsored for years, to the enlistment of persons through "proselytes of the gate" groups, where people participate in a "soft periphery" focusing primarily on Black culture. Such persons can often be led to Christ by showing them the spiritual underpinnings of Afro-American history and culture, and how our individual destinies are bound up in God's design for all of us.

Dr. Costen's statistics notwithstanding, Black Presbyterian churches are not growing at a rate that even begins to keep pace with population growth in their communities. Some observers have predicted that by the middle of the twenty-first century there will be no Black Presbyterians in the United States because of our poor performance in enlistment. If this is true, there is an urgent need to disprove the prediction by concentrating on evangelism and church growth. The desperate search for bodies to fill the pews and swell the offering plate can vulgarize the most enthusiastic evangelistic effort and must be avoided at all costs. But neither should we assume that our churches will go on until the Second Coming. It is possible for Black Presbyterianism to be snuffed out without any evidence that it ever existed, unless we become warm, inviting people who help others to catch a new vision of what it means to be a follower of Jesus Christ.

This last comment suggests the other equally important aspect of evangelism—the nurture of new converts in the bosom of the church. A common experience is to sign persons up on the new members roster only to see them fall away during the succeeding months. New-style evangelism will require that members of the congregation agree to sponsor and follow up new members. When they are drawn into families and intimate face-to-face groups, when we stop by to pick them up for church, or when we pray with them as they face the lonely task of taking up the yoke of Christ, we will find fewer new members straying from the fold. There is nothing novel about this kind of care and feeding of new members, but many fashionable churches have not been able to lay this burden for souls on their members. It will take a commitment to a new style to make our congregations evangelistic in the best sense of the term.

The issue of class discrimination cannot be evaded here. It is a problem for evangelism in many Presbyterian churches. As the lady in Hattiesburg said, "Pedestrians are too high class" for many who continue to reside in the vicinity of most of our Black churches. Whether justified or not, the reputation of Black Presbyterian congregations precedes them into the streets. The situation is not as deplorable as it was twenty years ago because of the general rise of Blacks into a higher socioeconomic status. But it is still true for many of our congregations that they rarely get an opportunity to present themselves to certain segments of the community because those segments never think about visiting a Presbyterian church. The word is out that "those folks have their noses in the air and don't want nobody who ain't in their class." The impression, as we have pointed out, is often erroneous. We no longer have a corner on the Black middle and upper classes.

Nevertheless, the impression persists. One of the purposes of the new style should be to break through this reputation of exclusivity and demonstrate that here are people who not only welcome all people to explore an exciting new form of Black Christianity with them but who also practice what they preach.

Evangelism has to do with the totality of the Christian commitment—the proclamation and demonstration of the power of God to redeem persons, groups, and institutions. The new members class is a critical opportunity for evangelism. When we introduce people to new-style discipleship we help them to see that joining a Black Presbyterian church means everything, from learning how to pray to working in a study group investigating economic alternatives to capitalism. When new members present themselves before the congregation to respond to the constitutional questions, they should receive a card showing that they are a registered voter as well as a membership card, a book on Black history and culture as well as a Bible, an assigned place in a small action-reflection group as well as a packet of offering envelopes. The time is past when we can give people the idea that all it takes to be a member of the Presbyterian Church is to believe in Christ and pay dues. We are a people on the move to the Kingdom of God. Those who join us on this journey come without racial, class, or any other kind of qualification, except they must be prepared to have Christ change their lives! They must be willing to consider what that change will be in the context of the history and culture of the Black community.

Outreach Into the Wider Community

This brings us to the third and final consideration of what new-style Black Presbyterianism would look like if we dared to try it. The question at the beginning of this chapter had to do with the middle-class orientation of the Black constituency of the Presbyterian Church and whether it is reasonable to expect that people like us will ever play a significant role in the empowerment of Black and Third World people. Are Black Presbyterians already too far along the path of renouncing the tradition of redemptive suffering through struggle that is basic to the Black religious experience, or can we really begin to forge a new style of life that will include involvement with forces working for the liberation of humankind?

One thing seems certain, and it is serious: Black Presbyterians will not voluntarily turn back the hands of the clock on themselves and their families. We will not return to the deprivation and misery of the long years of second class in the political economy of this nation, if it can be avoided. People who have worked hard all their lives to provide themselves and their children with a modicum of education and financial security as a hedge against the worst ravages of racism are not likely to give it all up in the interest of theories about what it takes to raise everybody's standard of living. Nor will such persons engage in a revolutionary movement that risks everything for some radical ideology, Christian or non-Christian. We have to face the fact that Christianity has made a difference in the world, but not *that* much of a difference en masse. Black Christians are just like others when it comes to rationalizing their advantages and finding pious reasons for substituting charity for a genuine redistribution of wealth and power.

But this does not mean that nothing can be done by people like us. Christians should always challenge one another to transcend the selfishness and egoism of the unredeemed world—even when the prospects for one hundred percent success are meager. We are continually surprised by grace. On the other hand, the serpentine wisdom of Christians, if not their innocence (Matt. 10:16), ought to make secular men and women who have believed the gospel find ways of changing the environment in order to change behavior, as well as the other way around. We are not certain of all that was in Jesus' mind when he told his followers to "make friends for yourselves by means of unrighteous mammon" (Luke 16:9), but it seems to be a practical counsel in the interest of the Kingdom. As we have already noted, Black folks are not shocked by such counsel. Those who are closest to the African religious heritage are no strangers to this kind of holy worldliness.

Our churches are, for the most part, still in the Black community. We are a part of that scene, whether we like it or not. It must be stressed that we stand or fall with others in that community—even after we have relocated our homes in the suburbs. It would behoove us to reach out to our neighbors, to take leadership in community organizations and institutions in search of a better life for everyone. It is clearly not wise to try to exist indefinitely on an island surrounded by polluted water. The self-interest of the churches, in addition to their expected sense of moral responsibility, should make them move out into the community, not just to operate a clothes hamper for the poor, or a hot-lunch program for senior citizens, but to help both groups register and vote, to present them regularly at city hall, to link them with other community forces in order to raise their level of self-esteem and aspiration by finding out what group power can do. It is the task of the Black Church not only to widen that island but to purify those waters so that life can blossom and flourish.

But the real key to outreach or missional style is not the conventional social action program of the local church, but Black ecumenism. The problem is not that Black Christians are uninvolved in our communities, they are—probably more than any other group. The problem is that they are out there divided, disorganized, and disoriented, as far as Black ethical and theological perspectives and as far as the churches as corporate institutions are concerned. A serene confidence and openness about sharing material and human resources with other churches—many of which will be less gifted—will be a mark of a new style of concern and outreach. Black churches in most areas need at least one congregation that will show that is is not interested in being "the biggest and the best" of anything, but wants to see congregations come together, pool their resources, and take charge of the community. Black Baptists are clannish and African Methodists are constantly in a whirlwind of denominational activities that pull people away from the local community, but someone needs to make an attempt to promote a Black ecumenism as the last best hope for the preservation of Afro-American culture. Black Presbyterian churches are prime candidates for this role because many of us have a wealth of talent for cooperative missional ventures and we are likely to be supported by the denomination in this kind of outreach. Nor is it necessary to waste time wooing reluctant Baptists and Methodists. In many communities Holiness and Pentecostal congregations are becoming open to others who respect them and are sincere in their desire for cooperation. Their younger and better-educated clergy are no less progressive than those of the older churches. There is often a "wait and see" attitude among the more established congregations. Once the broader ecumenical venture shows promise, many of them will come along.

None of the things we talked about in the 1960s and still need in the 1980s can be effectively implemented by a single congregation working alone: Black economic development, an independent Black political base, alternative elementary schools meeting in churches, family counseling centers, a Black United Fund, regular financial and political support for the liberation movements in Southern Africa. The issues are too large; the problems, too demanding. Instead of a ten-member social action committee, meeting once a month and trying to take on the world, the new style will be for the whole congregation to begin worshiping with, meeting with, and planning with two or three other churches. In such a manner it will be possible to apply the full weight of the churches against structures of power which determine life or death in our communities. Some group of laity must have the vision, theological perspective, and discipline to take the initiative and demonstrate what the Holy Spirit can do across denominational lines when we open ourselves to one another and the needs of the community. Black Presbyterian laity, operating out of new-style discipleship, should provide this kind of ecumenical leadership to the Black Church.

Educating White Folks

We cannot end this book without recognizing that Black Presbyterians belong to an overwhelmingly white denomination and we have some responsibility for white brothers and sisters. What is that responsibility?

We believe that Black Presbyterians ought to expect white churches to open themselves to the Black experience, to seek cooperation in joint mission where feasible, but not to encumber us with a white agenda when critical attention is needed on Black problems. Of course, there are no Black problems that are not connected in some way with white power, but there are levels of immediacy. We have our responsibilities in the ongoing work of the presbytery, but it makes no sense for white people to expect a small Black congregation to supply its best people to every committee of presbytery needing representatives, when most of them could be performing urgently needed tasks elsewhere. The new-style congregation will think of itself as presbytery's strategic outpost in the Black community. When it performs well it plays a role that no white congregation could play. It needs to be freed to play that role.

This does not mean that we should ask white brothers and sisters to give us their prayers and dollars and get out of our way. It means, rather, that the presbytery and the Black congregations should negotiate a proportionate allocation of time, resources, and energy from Blacks, if they are indeed to be the vanguard into an extremely difficult frontier of ministry. We are then able to open a way for white Presbyterians to take specific assignments and responsibilities on that part of the frontier where the two worlds—one Black and the other white—meet and, more often, collide.

Interracial cooperation is not just a routine affair requiring only good intentions on both sides and knowing how to "slap five." White Christians, after all these years, still need to be educated. They need to know more than they do today about Black culture and the ethos of the Black church and community. How that education takes place and what one does with it after it is acquired is a complicated question that deserves more discussion than we can give here. It should, however, be said that white people need to expose themselves to Blackenization no less than they have always expected Blacks to "act white" in order to be accepted. By Blackenization we do not mean some occasion when handclapping, foot-stomping, and eyeball-rolling become the Sambo-like imitation mistaken for "really getting down" with Black folks. Nothing could kill a partnership between our churches more quickly!

Blackenization refers here to sensitivity, knowledge, immersion in Black culture. It involves reading, directed observation, listening and entering into dialogue, and gradually contracting collaborative arrangements with Black congregations (not necessarily Presbyterian) to deal with issues and problems that crisscross the communities and call for joint operations. Such processes can be simultaneous. That is to say, we do not have to wait for something else to happen before we can be about this kind of cooperative strategy and action. One does well, of course, to proceed with deliberate speed with people who are mature, sincere Christians, people who are prepared to take risks with each other and to trust the Holy Spirit to bring mutual forgiveness, to make love cover a multitude of sins on both sides.

All of this is to say that new-style Black Presbyterianism will involve a new posture toward white people. It will be neither standoffish nor slavishly accommodating. It will negotiate reciprocal relations with white Presbyterians in behalf of liberation and reconciliation seen as two sides of a single coin. The new style means working on strategic partnership for the serious purposes of the Kingdom of God and, in the process, being open to a new understanding of love which includes justice. This partnership between Black and white churches is not just for "fun and fellowship," to "get white folks straightened out," or simply "to do what is expected of us as good Presbyterians." It is to enter into a quest for the unity of the body of Christ through mission together. It is to go together into the world, fully cognizant of the differences of culture, theological perspectives, and even mission priorities, but working out those differences and understandings as we go.

As I look back on what happened to Inez and Tom Jones, with whom we began this book, I feel—sad to say—that I must take some responsibility for not helping them understand what I have tried to say here. It *is* possible to keep one's integrity as a Black believer in a predominantly white congregation. It *is* possible to be Black and at the same time a loving, enthusiastic participant in a predominantly white denomination. But only if one bears witness to what God has given to Black Christians for all people to share. Only is one is willing, upon that rich heritage, to build a new style of life that gives hope for the interracial, interethnic, international Church that is breaking upon the world in advance of God's coming Kingdom.

Epilogue

It will be obvious to those who have stayed with us all the way that what this book proposes, as the advertisements of one of the car manufacturers say, is not for everyone. Only a minority of Presbyterians, perhaps only those who belong to or see purpose in a group like Black Presbyterians United, will agree that appreciation of the history and tradition of Black Christianity in America is critical for a proper understanding of what it should mean to be a Black Presbyterian. An even smaller minority will agree that such knowledge implies an obligation to adopt a new cultural vocation and life-style.

Most Christians, whether Black or white, find it much easier to fall in with the value system and life-style of the society at large. Our souls may be stirred and our hearts lifted up in our pews on Sunday morning. But Monday morning is a different kettle of fish. We get along best in this world by swimming with the current. So why should anyone take on a form of discipleship that will require a way of living that is sure to add problems to the already difficult business of professing religious faith in a smugly secular world?

To all who may come to such a conclusion after seriously considering what we have been contending for, we express gratitude for their having come this far with us. We respect their judgment and wish them well as they seek to prove their membership in this church in some other way. But we have no apology for making you feel uncomfortable if you are someone for whom Black Presbyterianism is nothing more than "social caucusing," and Christian discipleship no more than making a financial pledge and going to church. However, indulge us for one final flashback to Scripture.

Old man Joshua must be forgiven a certain amount of boasting about the accomplishments of Israel under his leadership. Ordained by Moses himself, he had shown admirable leadership ability and tactical skill. He had led the tribes across the Jordan, broken the power of the Canaanites, and settled his people with a reasonable amount of prosperity and security from their enemies (Josh. 14 to 18).

"Behold," he said to the leaders, "I have allotted to you as an inheritance for your tribes those nations that remain, along with all the nations that I have already cut off, from the Jordan to the Great Sea in the west."

No longer were they a band of fugitive slaves, straggling out of the desert, fighting for territorial rights against a people who looked down their noses at Israel's strange mountain God and their crude nomadic culture. If they had not yet quite "arrived" under Joshua, they were certainly on their way and could take pride and satisfaction "that not one thing has failed of all the good things which the LORD your God promised concerning you" (Josh. 23:14). Their position among the people west of the Jordan held promise for years to come. They were out of the wilderness at last.

But it was precisely for these reasons that Joshua felt it necessary to assemble the tribes, remind them of whence they had come since Egypt, and most important of all, warn them of the temptations of the good life, the idolatries of people who have come a long way—much of it on the backs of those who have gone before.

There were, in that gathering at Shechem, many who were wavering in their minds about the gods of the lands they sought. The lords of this rich earth, flowing with milk and honey, could not be as bad as Joshua had made out, tottering on his last legs and unable to enjoy the pleasures of younger years. Why not return to those gods their ancestors served across the Jordan, or turn to the gods of the people in whose land they were now settled? Why continue to placate this jealous, disciplinarian God of Moses and Joshua whose commandments were so burdensome and way of life so demanding?

Sensing their vacillation, Joshua admonished them:

> If you be unwilling to serve the LORD, choose this day whom you will serve, whether the gods your fathers served in the region beyond the River, or the gods of the Amorites in whose land you dwell; but as for me and my house, we will serve the LORD. (Josh. 24:15)

Life-style has to do with the gods one chooses to serve. Black Presbyterians must choose this day whom they will serve: the gods of bourgeois materialism and complacency, the reigning demons of suburban Shangri-las, the middle-management swivel chair in some corporate empire that imposes its own life-style, the make-believe world of Saturday night partying and Sunday morning golf, the Jack and Jill merry-go-round for children who don't know what enduring values have been sacrificed for their momentary pleasure, and the interminable round of cocktail parties with their predictable small talk about new houses, cars, fur coats, and vacations in Europe. Will it be these gods of the Black middle class, or the God of Biblical faith?

The question is of utmost seriousness. It is not something we can leave to chance, or to some democratic process where children have as much to say about the family life-style as their parents. Black people survived enslavement, discrimination and segregation, exploitation and impoverishment, by being faithful to the living God and determining to follow a way of life that was obedient to Christ and his church. We made choices for our families before it became fashionable for everyone to do his or her "own thing." The time has come, in the interest of the survival of Afro-American ethnicity and the values of the Black Christian community, to return to the faithful and disciplined life of a family that knows the difference between idols and the true God.

New-style Black Presbyterianism may sound to some like nothing more than a warmed-over version of the "old-time religion" of parents and grandparents, a return to the fundamentalistic dogma and high-handed authoritarianism of the last century. That is an erroneous assumption. We have advocated a return to roots—to a tradition that emphasizes independence, pragmatic spirituality, and Black liberation—in order to reclaim what is worth reclaiming, and then to go on blazing new paths toward the Kingdom of God.

We have indicated the main outline of a Black Christian life-style. We have pleaded for something different from vague, pointless denominationalism or race consciousness. Unless the Black members of this church demonstrate how being Black and Presbyterian are mutually valuable and enriching experiences which point toward a heritage and a hope that can make a difference in this world, there is no logical reason why any Black person would want to belong to this church which has ignored us for most of its existence.

In the final analysis, ordinary members of our congregations will have to decide whether or not they need to be this serious about being Black and Presbyterian, and if so, what style of life they are prepared to adopt for these times. We who are their ordained leaders can only speak for ourselves and pray that others may follow our example. It remains to be seen whether we ourselves are ready to stand forth and say with Joshua, "As for me and my house, we will serve the LORD."

Questions for Discussion

Chapter 1. ON BEING HUMAN—IN GENERAL
                AND IN PARTICULAR

1. Why is it so important to get our bearings in talking about race and religion by coming to some understanding about what is a human being? What analogies come to mind when theologians speak of "the family of God"?

2. What are the advantages and dangers of being color-blind in the real world? How does one have a "due sense" of differences without creating unnecessary alienation?

3. Compare Babel and Pentecost. What gifts did God give to the new church of the Gentiles which made it a pluralistic community ready to evangelize the world?

Chapter 2. WHAT IS BLACK CHRISTIANITY?

1. We need to be sure we understand about how Blacks first became Christians. What were some of the characteristics of African religions? Did they help or hinder Christianity?

2. Why do you think the church lost influence in the Black community before Dr. King came along? In what ways are we in that situation again today?

3. What do you think of the author's definition of Black Christianity? How would you describe it to someone from another country who knew nothing about church life in the United States?

Chapter 3. BLACK PEOPLE AND PRESBYTERIANISM

1. Go back and ask yourself: What does it mean to be a Presbyterian? Look at the Confession of 1967, for example, and see if it helps you understand what Presbyterians believe.

2. Who were some of the early pioneers and leaders of your congregation? How did they help or hinder this odyssey of Black Presbyterians from obscurity to national visibility and effectiveness?

3. In view of this brief sketch of Black Presbyterian history, how would you define Black Presbyterianism? What was the need for caucusing and how does it contribute to a more profound understanding of the Reformed faith?

Chapter 4. THE MIDDLE-CLASS BLACK CHURCH
AND THE IDENTITY CRISIS

1. To what extent has the author accurately stated the case for the attitudes of most Black people in your congregation? What exceptions or corrections would you suggest?

2. List some of the "meaningful differences" between Black and white congregations as you have observed them. How can those differences be "usefully traded" in order to make both churches more faithful and effective?

3. What do you understand by the "identity crisis"? Has it happened to you? If so, tell how it happened. If not, why not?

Chapter 5. RESOURCES OF THE BLACK CHRISTIAN TRADITION

1. Reread the details about Inez Jones in the Introduction. How would you describe her problem? How would you advise her if you were her friend?

2. Is there a Black Presbyterians United group in your area? If not, why not? What should be the main purpose and goal of such an organization?

3. Look at what the author calls the five resources of the Black Christian tradition in terms of your own congregation.

What is present and what is missing in your opinion? What can be done to strengthen these values in your own personal life and in your congregation?

Chapter 6. TOWARD A NEW STYLE OF BLACK
             PRESBYTERIANISM

1. This is a long chapter and may need to be discussed at more than one time. Considering the book as a whole, what do you think the author is trying to do in this final chapter? How successful is he?

2. Look at the Scriptural references that talk about wealth and privilege, including I Tim. 6:17–19. To what extent can comfortable people be expected to follow Jesus?

3. In discussing the elements of a new style, the author mentions leadership, congregational life, and outreach. Describe what is being called for. How do you think the challenges can be acted upon by you and your church?

EPILOGUE

1. After reading this book, how would you describe "the heritage" and "the hope" of being Black and Presbyterian?

2. How does being a Christian make a difference in your life? Tell what you believe your strengths are and where you need help.

3. A good way to end this study would be to develop a worship service for presenting what you have learned and by means of which the study group might bear witness to the entire congregation. What are some elements that would make such a service enlightening and inspiring?

Resources for Further Study

The following list of selected books and other resources excludes many different kinds of educational helps—maps, posters, multimedia kits, rituals, games, etc.—which have been developed in recent years to help congregations examine and nurture the concepts and values of Black and Third World history and culture dealt with in this book. Resource guides and bibliographies may be ordered from Joseph V. Nash, Director, Multiethnic/Multicultural Christian Education Resources Center, National Council of Churches, 705 Interchurch Center, 475 Riverside Dr., New York, N.Y. 10115.

Pastors and Christian education leaders should also consult *Afro-American Educational Materials, for Pre-Kindergarten Through High School, 1981–82*, AFRO-AM Distributing Co., 910 S. Michigan Ave., Suite 556, Chicago, Ill. 60605, and the JED Black Church Education Team, Rita Dixon, Director, Racial and Ethnic Ministries, Presbyterian Church in the U.S., 341 Ponce de Leon Ave., N.E., Atlanta, Ga. 30308.

One of the best teaching resources for local church use, beginning in September 1983, is the Faith Journey Series, a part of *Christian Education: Shared Approaches*, a project of Joint Educational Development. The lesson material is suitable for many non-Presbyterian congregations. For further information, write to Curriculum Services UPCUSA, P.O. Box 868 William Penn Annex, Philadelphia, Pa. 19105.

The books listed below were selected because they explain

and often expand upon many of the ideas of this book and provide additional study material. Most of them are available in paperback editions and are suitable for youth and adult lay readers. The other resources listed are recommended for adult study groups, church school classes, camps and conferences, etc.

Books

Carter, Harold A. *The Prayer Tradition of Black People.* Judson Press, 1976.

Cone, James H. *Black Theology and Black Power.* Seabury Press, 1969.

————. *My Soul Looks Back.* Abingdon Press, 1982.

Du Bois, W. E. B. *The Gift of Black Folk.* 1924. Washington Square Press, 1970.

————. *The Souls of Black Folk.* Fawcett Publications, 1961.

————. *The World and Africa.* International Publishers, 1978.

George, Carol V. R. *Segregated Sabbaths: Richard Allen and the Emergence of Independent Black Churches, 1760–1840.* Oxford University Press, 1973.

Harding, Vincent. *There Is a River: The Black Struggle for Freedom in America.* Harcourt Brace Jovanovich, 1981.

Jahn, Janheinz. *Muntu: An Outline of the New African Culture.* Grove Press, 1961.

Jones, William A. *God in the Ghetto.* Progressive Baptist Publishing House, 1979.

King, Martin L., Jr. *Strength to Love.* Collins-World Publishing Co., 1963.

————. *Where Do We Go from Here: Chaos or Community?* Harper & Row, 1967.

Levine, Lawrence W. *Black Culture and Black Consciousness.* Oxford University Press, 1977.

Lincoln, C. Eric, ed. *The Black Experience in Religion.* Doubleday & Co., 1974.

Lovell, John. *Black Song: The Forge and the Flame, The Story of How the Afro-American Spiritual Was Hammered Out.* Macmillan Co., 1972.

Marable, Manning. *Blackwater: Historical Studies in Race, Class Consciousness and Revolution.* Black Praxis Press, 1981.

Mbiti, John S. *African Religions and Philosophy.* Frederick A. Praeger, 1969.

McClain, William B. *Travelling Light: Pluralism and Pilgrimage.* Friendship Press, 1981.

Mitchell, Henry. *Black Belief: Folk Beliefs of Blacks in America and West Africa.* Harper & Row, 1975.

Murray, Andrew E. *Presbyterians and the Negro—A History.* Presbyterian Historical Society, 1966.

Roberts, J. Deotis. *Roots of a Black Future: Family and Church.* Westminster Press, 1980.

Smith, J. Alfred. *The Church in Bold Mission: A Guidebook on Black Church Development.* Southern Baptist Convention, 1977.

Thomas, Latta R. *Biblical Faith and the Black American.* Judson Press, 1976.

Thurman, Howard. *Deep River: Reflections on the Religious Insight of Certain of the Negro Spirituals.* Harper & Brothers, 1955.

————. *Jesus and the Disinherited.* Abingdon-Cokesbury Press, 1949.

Walker, Wyatt Tee. *Somebody's Calling My Name: Black Sacred Music and Social Change.* Judson Press, 1979.

Wilmore, Gayraud S., and Cone, James H. *Black Theology: A Documentary History, 1966–1979.* Orbis Books, 1979.

Woodson, Carter G. *The History of the Negro Church.* Associated Publishers, 1972.

Pamphlets, Portfolios, and Booklets

The Black Church in America. A special compendium issue of *Dollars and Sense*, June/July 1981. Eighteen articles and feature items containing statistics, etc., on the contemporary Black Church in the U.S.A. Order from National Publication Sales Agency, Inc., 840 E. 87th St., Suite 202, Chicago, Ill. 60619.

The Black Church in the 1980s. Lectures by Lawrence N. Jones from the Sixth Annual B. Moses James Colloquium on Black Religion, 1980. The Black Council of the Reformed Church in America, 1823 Interchurch Center, 475 Riverside Dr., New York, N.Y. 10115.

Black Presbyterians in Mission. An occasional publication of the Office of Black Mission Development, Program Agency, The United Presbyterian Church U.S.A., 1244F Interchurch Center, 475 Riverside Dr., New York, N.Y. 10115.

Black Presbyterians United: Report to the Session. A booklet edited by Clarence Cave containing workshop reports and addresses on renewing congregational life. Tenth Annual Conference of Black Presbyterians United, March 17–20, 1977. Order from Presbyterian Distribution Service, 935 Interchurch Center, 475 Riverside Dr., New York, N.Y. 10115.

A Design for Evangelism in the Black Presbyterian Church. A Resource of Black Presbyterians for Renewal and Growth by William G. Gillespie. Program Agency of The United Presbyterian Church U.S.A., the Second Cumberland Presbyterian Church, and the Presbyterian Church U.S. Order from PDS.

Dynamics of Church Growth. A Resource of Black Presbyterians for Renewal and Growth by Lonnie J. Oliver. Order from PDS.

Education and Religion. A social studies portfolio of prints featuring early and modern Black educators and religious leaders and their contributions to Black life. AFRO-AM Distributing Co., 1981.

Good News Among Black Youth. A Resource of Black Presbyterians for Renewal and Growth by Robert S. Wood and Gayle E. Wood. Order from PDS.

Great Kings of Africa. A portfolio of 14 full-color reprints of paintings with captions in tribute to the heritage of Afro-Americans. Anheuser-Busch, Inc., 2800 S. Ninth St., St. Louis, Mo. 63118.

Identity Crisis: Blacks in Predominantly White Denominations. Lectures by Gayraud S. Wilmore from the Second Annual B. Moses James Colloquium on Black Religion, 1976. The Black Council of the Reformed Church in America.

Lift Every Voice and Sing: A Collection of Afro-American Spirituals and Other Songs. Contains 151 pieces of music from Black religious experience. The Church Hymnal Corporation, 800 Second Ave., New York, N.Y. 10017.

Ministry Among Black Americans: Responding to a Need. A booklet of the Saint Meinrad School of Theology containing lectures by Edward Branch, Giles Conwill, Edward Braxton, and Gayraud S. Wilmore, 1977. Order from Saint Meinrad School of Theology, St. Meinrad, Ind. 47577.

Periscope I. A booklet of essays edited by Frank T. Wilson and Emily Gibbs in commemoration of 175 years of Black Presbyterianism. Order from PDS.

Reaching the Dropout Church Member. A Resource of Black Presbyterians for Renewal and Growth by L. Charles Gray. Order from PDS.

The Redemption of Africa and Black Religion. A pamphlet by St. Clair Drake on the story of the relationship between the Black Church and Africa. Institute of the Black World and the Third World Press, 7850 S. Ellis Ave., Chicago, Ill. 60619.

Soulfull Worship. A 160-page booklet by Clarence J. Rivers dealing with the question What is Black worship? An aid to creative and effective worship. National Office of Black Catholics, 1234 Massachusetts Ave., N.W., Suite 1004, Washington, D.C. 20005.

Audio-Visual Resources

Alex Haley: The Search for Roots. Color film, 18 mins., rental. Films for the Humanities, P.O. Box 2053, Princeton, N.J. 08540.

Black Religion I (The Church), *Black Religion II* (The Preacher). Filmstrips, 80–90 frames each, 12–17 mins., color, disc or cassettes. Scholastic Audiovisual Center, 904 Sylvan Ave., Englewood Cliffs, N.J. 07632.

Black Studies Resources Slide Series with Text. A set of over 450 source documents, prints, lithographs, drawings, early photographs, etc.; many focusing on Black religious history and culture. 465 slides, 118-page guide. Educational Design, Inc., 47 W. 13th St., New York, N.Y. 10011.

Conversations with Dr. Howard Thurman. A film about the great mystic and Black theologian discussing his early childhood as a grandson of slaves, his teaching career and pastorate in San Francisco. Rental. DDS Film Library, Association Films, 5797 New Peachtree Rd., Atlanta, Ga. 30340.

Dr. Martin Luther King, Jr.: An Amazing Grace. Color film, 62 mins., rental. McGraw-Hill Films, 110 15th St., Del Mar, Calif. 92014.

Ethnic Peoples Tape Cassettes, No. 5: Black Americans. Deals with many aspects of Black life and history, including the church civil rights movement, Dr. King, and Malcolm X. Filmstrip, cassette, teacher's manual and student exams. Educational Design, Inc., 47 W. 13th St., New York, N.Y. 10011.

Gift of the Black Folk. Color film, 16 mins., rental. Pyramid Films, Box 1048, Santa Monica, Calif. 90406.

Historical Interpretations of Negro Spirituals and Lift Every Voice and Sing. Record. Explains and demonstrates the use of spirituals as code messages for escaping slaves. Songs and narrated interpretations. AFRO-AM Distributing Co., 910 S. Michigan Ave., Suite 558, Chicago, Ill. 60605.

An Introduction to Gospel Song and Country Gospel Song. Set of two records demonstrating the early music of the Black Church which lies behind contemporary jazz and gospel. AFRO-AM Distributing Co., 910 S. Michigan Ave., Suite 558, Chicago, Ill. 60605.

New Roads to Faith: Black Perspectives in Church Education. Developed by Black theologian Yvonne V. Delk. Filmstrip packet contains two-part filmstrip, color, 317 frames plus credit frames, two audio-cassettes. Guide and script, 33 mins. Order from Curriculum Services UPCUSA, P.O. Box 868, William Penn Annex, Philadelphia, Pa. 19105.

The Smaller Churches: Repairers of the Breach. A two-part filmstrip, 26 mins., 213 frames, record. Developed by Union Seminary students to document social ministry of Harlem and Brooklyn storefront churches. Media-Modes, Inc., Cathedral Station, P.O. Box 466, New York, N.Y. 10025.

Two Black Churches (1975). Color film, 16mm., 20 mins. Center for Southern Folklore, 1216 Peabody Ave., P.O. Box 4081, Memphis, Tenn. 38104. *Let the Church Say, Amen!* Cokesbury Service Center, 201 Eighth Ave., S., Nashville, Tenn. 37202. Two studies presenting varied aspects of the Black religious tradition through churches in mission to their respective communities.